STUDENT LEARNING GUIDE

for use with

FOURTH EDITION

New Society

Sociology for the 21st Century

Prepared by Deborah Boutilier

THOMSON
*
NELSON

Australia   Canada   Mexico   Singapore   Spain   United Kingdom   United States

THOMSON

★

NELSON

**Student Learning Guide for use with New Society:
Sociology for the 21st Century, Fourth Edition**

by Robert J. Brym
Prepared by Deborah Boutilier

Editorial Director and Publisher:
Evelyn Veitch

Executive Editor:
Joanna Cotton

Acquisitions Editor:
Cara Yarzab

Marketing Manager:
Lenore Taylor

Developmental Editor:
Glen Herbert

Production Editor:
Julie van Veen

Proofreader:
Valerie Adams

Senior Production Coordinator:
Hedy Sellers

Creative Director:
Angela Cluer

Cover Design:
Andrew Adams

Cover Image:
© Bill Ross/CORBIS/ MAGMA

Printer:
Webcom

National Library of Canada Cataloguing in Publication Data

Boutilier, Deborah
    Student learning guide for use with New society : sociology for the 21st century, fourth edition / prepared by Deborah Boutilier.

ISBN 0-17-622485-8

1. Sociology—Problems, exercises, etc. I. Brym, Robert J., 1951–. New society. II. Title.

HM586.B79 2004 Suppl. 1   301
C2004-900745-9

Preface

How Can I Get the Most out of My Student Learning Guide?

This book is called a Student Learning Guide and not a Student Study Guide for some very specific reasons. Although it looks the same as other study guides that you might have used in the past, this supplemental learning tool is meant to act as a guide that will enhance your learning skills in the area of sociology, while at the same time providing the comprehensive understanding that you need in order to be successful in this course. Rather than merely testing your familiarity with the textbook or improving your memory retention, if used properly, this guide will also give you the self-confidence and knowledge that you will need in order to produce quality exams and research papers. More often than not, it is these important course requirements that determine your level of success or failure in any subject. Any student can study, but it's only the successful ones that can truly learn.

Your student learning guide is not too big or too heavy to carry in your knapsack or briefcase. Instead, it's easy to access and convenient to use wherever or whenever you choose to learn. I've designed it so that you can learn from it with or without the use of your textbook but it's important to remember that this guide should never be used as a substitute for your textbook, and that it works best when used in conjunction with your text. You'll notice that your learning guide mirrors the most important parts of the textbook, but also adds supplemental material to enhance your studying. From students that I've taught over the years, I've found that bringing your learning guide to class and highlighting the topics that the instructor discusses during lectures is an excellent way to gain a greater understanding of the most important concepts that are likely to appear on a test or exam. Additionally, writing in your learning guide makes reviewing material for an exam much easier.

Your student learning guide is also simplistic in form and it attempts, through a variety of ways, to guide your learning. You are ultimately responsible for actually accumulating and retaining educational knowledge; however, this book will help you to facilitate your learning so that it becomes something enjoyable, not stressful. I've been a student for most of my life and probably for more years than you've been alive, and I've tried to draw on some of the experiences that I've had as a student and instructor to help you have a greater understanding of how sociological theories really work in everyday life. I've had a totally awesome time creating this book and I sincerely hope that you have just as much fun using it. Carry it with you in your knapsack and pull it out when you get a chance — in between classes, over morning coffee, or even while waiting for the bus. You'll be amazed at how much this little book can offer, but even more amazed at how much it can make you think!

True/False and Multiple Choice Questions

Objective-type questions not only test how much you remember from the textbook, they also make you think about what you've learned and what makes you remember what you've learned. From these questions, try to develop your learning skills and identify the tricks that you can use to help you retain material from the textbook. These questions are not designed simply to test your memory recall. These are tools that can help you learn. Your scores here should be a good indication of how well you understand each chapter. If your scores are not good (i.e., less than 60 percent), reread the chapter and try again. These questions are especially designed to help you prepare for any upcoming objective examinations and should act as good indicators of your potential performance levels.

Critical Thinking Questions

The study of sociology can be defined as the method by which ordinary people, like you and me, strive to understand what is happening to them and their society. Systematic observation of the structures, institutions, and forces in society encourages us to look beyond the strictly personal and individual events that affect our lives, allowing us to use our critical thinking skills to see the world from a different, more global perspective. The need for such understanding is urgent at this present historical moment when change is rapid and the future is uncertain. Because of these reasons and more, unprecedented opportunities to build a better world and improve the quality of life for many people lie ahead. You can capitalize on those opportunities and the study of sociology can help. By taking this course and reading both your textbook and your student learning guide, you'll explore how society works, how it doesn't work, and the things that you can do to change it. By investigating sociological perspectives and developing a sociological imagination, you can gain the potential to change the world.

The critical thinking questions included at the end of each chapter require you to adopt a more subjective and critical attitude to the issues at hand. While it is important to learn about sociology, it is equally important to learn how to use the skills of a sociologist. It's great to grasp the meanings of the theories, but it's even better to be able to apply those theories to the real-life situations that confront us daily. Subjective learning gives us as much of an opportunity to enrich our understanding as objective learning, but it requires that we use a different set of skills. That's where the imagination part comes in. When you attempt to answer these questions, try to picture yourself in the situations, and don't be afraid to let your ideas come forth, regardless of how "off the wall" they may seem to you or to others. Critical thinking is the key to understanding all of the different facets that one idea or theory can have. Let your imagination go crazy — you'll be surprised at what you come up with!

Tips for Better Learning

1. Identify the kind of learner that you are! Are you a visual, auditory, or kinesthetic learner? Once you've identified your learning style (Student Services or Counselling should be able to help you with this), work on developing your reading, writing, and study skills. If your university or college offers workshops — attend them! Usually, the Student Services or Student Development centre offers classes in time management, relaxation, exam anxiety, note taking, essay writing, and study skills. Though some may charge a nominal fee for these services, they are usually well worth the money and can often be invaluable to your education.

2. Use your library and all the talented people who work there. Most college and university libraries offer tours and information sessions that acquaint you with the many services they provide.

3. Get organized! Creating a schedule that you can live with often determines not only the success of your academic year, it also allows you to make the best of your leisure time as well. A social life is just as important as an academic life, so make sure that you include some recreational time in your planner. A good schedule is a realistic one. By scheduling time away from studies, you allow yourself to have some fun without worrying about upcoming assignments.

4. Get computer literate — learn how to use the Internet and the World Wide Web. This can cut your essay writing time in half. Most schools offer free two- or three-hour workshops on how to research on the Internet. I always advise my students to take a basic word-processing course as an elective credit in their degree program. That way not only do they earn a credit, they develop a very worthwhile skill.

5. Improve your reading skills. Start out by substituting television with just a half hour of reading instead. It doesn't matter what you read, as long as you get into the habit. Even if it's recreational reading, it will enhance your reading skills, which will help improve the reading skills that you use for studying.

6. Learn to type!

7. Form a study group — many students find that this is a great way to study and reinforce information that they have learned. It also allows them to interact with each other and to get to know their classmates better.

A Word to the Educators Who Use This Guide

Having taught a variety of sociology courses over the past decade, I am well acquainted with the enormous amount of preparation time required to effectively present material that students will clearly understand and retain. This Student Learning Guide has been designed to provide thought-provoking material for students, as well as teachers. The objective-type questions make great quizzes and the critical thinking questions will facilitate good group discussions and seminar presentations. The websites are great and they encourage the student to learn more about the topics that are associated with those covered in the textbook.

About the Author

Deborah Boutilier teaches in the Interdisciplinary Studies and Access Division at Niagara College in Welland, Ontario. She holds a Master of Arts in Sociology from SUNYAB and a Master of Education from Brock University. She is currently completing a doctoral degree in Education at OISE/UT, where she is also employed as a graduate researcher.

Acknowledgements

I'm honoured to have been selected to write the Student Learning Guide to such an excellent textbook, and am mindful of the talented individuals that made this journey possible. I am very lucky to have had Dr. Ray Boily, Rob Pepler, Judy Ferron, Diana Notton, and Betty Fishbait play such an important role in this endeavour. I am forever grateful to Robert Brym, who is an extraordinary academician, and for the incredible talents of Cara Yarzab, Glen Herbert, and Daryn DeWalt of Nelson. This, more than any other, has been for the students that have taught me so much over the years, among them, my brother Russell. Every once in a while, when I have the time, I like to think that I've taught them a few things too — the least of which is that school should never have to hurt.

Table of Contents

Chapter 1

Introducing Sociology

Chapter Introduction

The goal of this chapter is to guide you to a place in your mind that will allow you to think and learn about sociology. There's a really good chance that you have already "done" sociology, but have not been aware that your thoughts and behaviours were shaped by societal influences. How often do you question the "invisible" actions and reactions that surround the seemingly routine activity of meeting a friend for coffee? Do you ever wonder where the coffee beans came from or the daily wage of the people who picked them? Is having coffee with a friend simply about the process of drinking coffee or are there other, more important reasons for getting together? Does it matter if you have tea instead of coffee? In developing an understanding of how to think sociologically, you may often find yourself thinking and questioning things that you would usually take for granted. The process involved in thinking and questioning is almost always a good thing and the study of sociology will make you feel better about trying to understand the complexities that surround the society in which you live.

Sometimes in the attempt to understand a new body of knowledge, you get so caught up in trying to determine what the subject is all about that you often fail to think about what the subject is not. Brym's explanation of sociology offers a solid foundation on which to begin your understanding of this discipline by providing an excellent review of what sociology is and couching it within the differences that exist between sociology and other disciplines of investigation. By self-disclosing his own beginnings as a somewhat hesitant sociologist, Brym invites you to become a critical thinker as you discover the many facets that create your world.

Learning Objectives

At the conclusion of this chapter, you should be able to discuss or write about the following without having to rely on the textbook:

1. Durkheim showed that even apparently nonsocial and antisocial actions are influenced by social structures. Specifically, he showed how levels of social solidarity affect suicide rates.

2. Due to the rise in youth suicide, the pattern of suicide rates in Canada today is not exactly the same as in Durkheim's France. Nevertheless, Durkheim's theory explains the contemporary Canadian pattern well.

3. Sociologists analyze the connection between personal troubles and social structures.

4. Sociologists analyze the influence of three levels of social structure on human action: microstructures, macrostructures, and global structures.

5. Values and theories suggest which sociological research questions are worth asking and how the parts of society fit together. A theory is a tentative explanation of some aspect of social life. It states how and why specific facts are connected. Research is the process of carefully observing social reality to assess the validity of a theory.

6. There are four major theoretical traditions in sociology. Functionalism analyzes how social order is supported by macrostructures. The conflict paradigm analyzes how social inequality is maintained and challenged. Symbolic interactionism analyzes how meaning is created when people communicate in microlevel settings. Feminism focuses on the social sources of patriarchy in both macro and micro settings.

7. The rise of sociology was stimulated by the scientific, industrial, and democratic revolutions.

8. The Postindustrial Revolution is the technology-driven shift from manufacturing to service industries and the consequences of that shift for virtually all human activities.

9. The causes and consequences of postindustrialism form the great sociological puzzle of our time. The tension between autonomy and constraint, prosperity and inequality, and diversity and uniformity are among the chief interests of sociology today.

Quiz Questions

True or False?

1. Sociologists examine the connection between personal troubles and social relations.
    True or False

2. Because we are social beings that interact with others and the world around us, it is impossible to distinguish the social cause of phenomena from the physical and emotional causes.
    True or False

3. According to Durkheim, the Protestant belief that "religious doubts can be reduced and a state of grace assured if people work diligently" was called the Protestant work ethic.
    True or False

4. The feminist paradigm holds that male domination and female subordination are determined biologically.
    True or False

5. Symbolic interactionism stresses that people help to create their social circumstances and do not merely react to them.
    True or False

6. Durkheim argued that suicide rates vary due to differences in the degree of social solidarity in different groups.
    True or False

7. Because it is hard to study large groups in society, sociologists must also study individuals.
    True or False

8. It is believed that Jews are less likely to commit suicide than Christians because centuries of persecution have turned them into a group that is more defensive and tightly knit.
    True or False

9. Sociologists call relatively stable patterns of social relations "social structures."
    True or False

10. You are more likely to find a job faster if you understand "the strength of weak ties" in microstructural settings.
    True or False

Multiple Choice

1. Which of the following is not true?
   a. Sociologists examine the connection between personal troubles and social relations.
   b. Sociology originated at the time of the Age of Enlightenment
   c. The causes of human behaviour lie partly in the patterns of social relations that surround people.
   d. Sociological research is often motivated by the desire to improve the social world.

2. At the end of the nineteenth century, _____ demonstrated that suicide is more than just an individual act of depression.
   a. Marx
   b. Engels
   c. Durkheim
   d. Weber

3. _____ structures lie outside and above the national level.
   a. International
   b. Macro
   c. Global
   d. Micro

4. This chapter showed that diminished _____ relations have powerfully influenced suicide rates.
   a. psychological
   b. social
   c. religious
   d. intimate

5. A _____ is a tentative explanation of some aspect of social life that states how and why certain facts are related.
   a. sociological question
   b. theory
   c. null hypothesis
   d. statement

6. Compared to the youth of the 1960s, young people today are _____ likely to take their own lives if they happen to find themselves in the midst of a personal crisis.
   a. more
   b. less
   c. not at all
   d. equally

7. Half a century ago, the great American sociologist _____ called the ability to see the connection between personal troubles and social structures the "sociological imagination."
   a. Karl Marx
   b. Emile Durkheim
   c. Max Weber
   d. C. Wright Mills

8. The term *sociology* was coined by the French social thinker _____.
   a. Auguste Comte
   b. Emile Durkheim
   c. Talcott Parsons
   d. Jean Jacques Rouseau

9. Which of the following is not a commonly accepted basis for knowing that something is "true" in our everyday lives?
   a. Qualification
   b. Overgeneralization
   c. Internal logic
   d. Ego-defence

10. _____ are ideas about what is right and wrong.
   a. Norms
   b. Laws
   c. Folkways
   d. Values

11. _____ suggests that re-establishing equilibrium in society can best solve most social problems.
   a. Feminism
   b. Symbolic interactionism
   c. Conflict theory
   d. Functionalism

12. Class conflict lies at the centre of _____'s ideas.
   a. Karl Marx
   b. Emile Durkheim
   c. George Herbert Mead
   d. John Porter

13. _____ refers to the technology-driven shift from manufacturing to service industries and the consequences of that shift on virtually all human activities.
   a. The Industrial Revolution
   b. The Technological Revolution
   c. The Postindustrial Revolution
   d. Alvin Toffler's "Future Shock"

14. "The proper place for women is in the home. That's the way it's always been." This statement represents knowledge based on _____.
    a. casual observation
    b. overgeneralization
    c. tradition
    d. selective observation

15. What does Yorick's dilemma tell us?
    a. That hard work pays off.
    b. That life is finite.
    c. That people live on in memories, after their death.
    d. That true friendship never dies.

Critical Thinking

1. Durkheim's study of suicide in France remains a landmark work in the field of sociology. Often touted as the supremely antisocial and nonsocial act, suicide is thought to be a highly individual act that occurs outside the realm of social forces. When people that we know or celebrities take their own life, our first reaction is to try and understand why. How many times have you tried to determine the motive behind a suicide? Have you ever thought that suicide is inextricably linked to social forces? Though many theories exist, will we ever discover the story behind Kurt Cobain's tragic death? Why would he choose to end his life at a time when it seemed as though his life was perfect? What are the social factors that you think contributed to his death?

2. A good understanding of the fundamental theories is an absolute necessity that can often determine your success in any sociology course. For this exercise, consider the existence of prostitution in society. Remember that it is legal in some countries (Germany and France) but illegal in most others. How would a structural functionalist, a conflict theorist, a feminist, and a symbolic interactionist explain prostitution?

3. According to the work of Mark Granovetter (1973), you are likely to find a job faster if you understand the "strength of weak ties" in microstructural settings. Do you agree with his findings? Do you know people who got great jobs because of their "connections"? How helpful is it to know someone when it comes to finding meaningful work?

4. Sociology is becoming increasingly reliant on the knowledge-worker, and the ability to acquire, retain, and apply a variety of information is an important tool for anyone that plans to enter the workforce. Since you're using this learning guide, you are probably enrolled at a college or university that will help you with the processes that are involved in understanding and retaining knowledge. To what extent do you think that your time spent in a formal educational setting will assist you in obtaining the career of your dreams? Examine your reasons for being in school. How will you feel if, after you graduate, you don't get the job that you've spent so much time and money preparing for?

Web Links

Sociologist at Large
http://ryoung001.homestead.com/
This is an excellent site that introduces you to sociology in a number of different ways. It's a free service (although they do mention donations) that also allows you submit questions that you have about sociology.

Social Studies
http://www.ncss.org
This website, produced by the National Council for Social Studies, offers both educators and students a variety of information from the world of social studies. Of special interest to you might be the section called "Student News and Views." It's great to see how students from around the world study their societies.

Electronic Journal of Sociology
http://www.sociology.org
An incredibly valuable free website that offers you access to some excellent online sociological journals, as well as some instructional material should you ever think about publishing!

Directory of Social Science
http://dir.yahoo.com/Social_Science/Sociology/
Make sure to add this one to your list of favourites — full access to virtually every topic imaginable in the quest for sociological information.

Solutions

True or False?

1. T
2. F
3. F
4. F
5. T
6. T
7. F
8. T
9. T
10. T

Multiple Choice

1. B
2. C
3. C
4. C
5. B
6. A
7. D
8. A
9. C
10. D
11. D
12. A
13. C
14. C
15. B

Chapter 2

Research Methods

Chapter Introduction

Now that you've got a very basic understanding of what sociology is and how it can affect your life, it's time to think about the ways in which sociologists gather the information that attempts to describe your world. This is often easier said than done because you're probably not used to thinking about the creation or determination of social factors. Just like other scientists, social scientists attempt to discover evidence that can be used to explain how or why our social realities exist. Although it's very different from the methods used in other sciences (either natural or social), social research is all about the purposeful, systematic, and rigorous collection of information. It's often difficult in sociology because we're trying to gather data that will help us to predict the behaviour of human beings and, as you probably already know, it's often hard to understand people, let alone predict what they're going to do next!

This chapter reveals some of the most popular methods of collecting meaningful information from and about people. While you're reading your textbook, listening to your instructor, or working with this guide, I want you to start thinking "sociologically." Instead of just believing everything that you hear or read about, start questioning where the information comes from. If you read the newspapers, is one paper more credible than another? Do you automatically believe the messages that television commercials are trying to get across? Have you ever wondered where those four out of five dentists come from or how huge corporations determine how many people prefer Coke instead of Pepsi? Often, it's sociologists that gather this information, and when you begin to critically evaluate the information that you hear or read, you'll get an idea of just how interesting the life of a social researcher can be. The critical thinking questions in this chapter really give you the opportunity to start thinking like a sociologist.

Learning Objectives

At the conclusion of this chapter, you should be able to discuss or write about the following, without having to rely on the textbook:

1. Research methods are ways of getting evidence to test suppositions about the world around us. Behind the various techniques (e.g., experiments, interviews) we use to obtain evidence and expand our knowledge of the social world, we must recognize important assumptions about such things as facts, objectivity, and truth.

2. Science is one of several sources of knowledge. Like other kinds of knowledge, scientific knowledge can be wrong. However, unlike other ways of knowing, science incorporates explicit methods designed to reduce error in what is currently accepted as scientific knowledge. Evidence must be systematically collected and rigorously evaluated.

3. Good science integrates both good theory and good research. The latter two are inseparable. Theories are ideas about how the world works or claims about how to explain or understand the recurring, patterned nature of human activity.

4. Evidence is crucial to developing, revising, or discarding theoretical claims. In comparison with the evidence available in the natural sciences, the evidence available to social scientists presents added complexity because of the meaningful character of human social action. People, unlike molecules, assign meaning to their actions and to the actions of others.

5. Sociologists have devised many useful methods to obtain evidence about the social world. Observation and questioning are the two principal techniques, although each of them is conducted using a variety of formats, including experiments, surveys, participant observation, and interviews.

6. Good research adds to our knowledge of the world around us. Such knowledge expands our opportunities and options. Sociological knowledge helps either in solving social problems or by sensitizing us to our collective human condition, expanding our social horizons.

Quiz Questions

True or False?

1. Values have the potential to bias or distort observations, and both the natural and the social sciences must guard against distortion. If the scientific method is defined as a set of practices or procedures for testing the validity of knowledge claims, both chemists and sociologists could be seen as "doing" science.
   True or False

2. Experiments are the hallmark of scientific research.
   True or False

3. Among the rules of scientific method working to enhance objectivity and eliminate personal bias are critical scrutiny and full disclosure.
   True or False

4. To understand the meaning of social action requires being able, at least in principle, to participate in the social activity of which the action is a part.
   True or False

5. Only a scientific system of knowledge invariably produces truth, unerringly generating eternal accuracy.
   True or False

6. When data are being collected, individuals can act as informants to report information that pertains not only to themselves, but additionally to some group or unit about which they have information.
   True or False

7. Social research involves systematically collecting theoretically relevant data in a way that minimizes error. It helps us to distinguish sociology from mere opinion.
   True or False

8. Science is founded on facts derived from direct observation.
   True or False

9. A variable is a measurable concept that can have more than one value.
   True or False

10. Randomization lies at the heart of experimental design. Using a random procedure, people in an experiment are assigned to an experimental condition on the basis of chance.
    True or False

Multiple Choice

1. "Men have higher annual incomes than women." In this statement, gender is the_____ variable.
    a. independent
    b. dependent
    c. confounding
    d. mediating

2. _____ are designed to reduce the likelihood that we are dealing in artifacts, while enhancing the likelihood that we have reproducible evidence.
    a. Theories
    b. Hypotheses
    c. Research methods
    d. Scientific facts

3. The criminal justice system minimizes error through _____.
    a. the discovery of precedents
    b. evidence and presumptions of innocence
    c. the penal code
    d. the right to a speedy trial

4. _____ refers to accuracy or relevancy.
    a. Reliability
    b. Internal consistency
    c. Random selection
    d. Validity

5. Like all human activities, the social practice of science is influenced by _____.
    a. common sense
    b. subjectivity
    c. expertise/authority
    d. scientific laws

6. A(n) _____ variable is presumed to affect other variables.
    a. dependent
    b. independent
    c. moderating
    d. confounding

7. Social scientists use the term _____ effect when referring to changes in people's behaviour caused by their awareness of being studied.

    a. Brisbane

    b. Schmanker

    c. Hawthorne

    d. Holland

8. By imagining yourself in the role of another, you come to appreciate someone else's point of view. This process, called "taking the role of the other," is reflected in the work of _____.

    a. Max Weber

    b. George Herbert Mead

    c. Erving Goffman

    d. none of the above

9. Which of the following is not appropriate when designing questionnaires?

    a. assuming the people understand what you are asking

    b. assuming that people know the answer to questions

    c. assuming the people will give valid answers to questions

    d. all of the above

10. We must be cautious in generalizing the results of laboratory experiments to non-laboratory situations. This concern is technically expressed as a problem of _____ validity, or the degree to which experimental findings remain valid in non-laboratory situation.

    a. face

    b. external

    c. internal

    d. empirical

11. A _____ is an unverified but testable knowledge claim about the social world.

    a. hypothesis

    b. theory

    c. paradigm

    d. statement

12. _____ was one of the first sociologists to address the issue of interaction as a problem of social research. He argued that our interactions with other people draw upon meanings.

    a. Robert Gale

    b. Emile Durkheim

    c. Karl Marx

    d. Max Weber

13. According to the textbook, which is not a feature of social science research?

    a. Research results are confronted by the critical skepticism of other scientists.

    b. Social theory guides, either directly or indirectly, the evidence gathered.

    c. Social facts or findings are presented in a meaningful way.

    d. Evidence is systematically collected and analyzed.

14. David Hume disputed the popular argument of his day that science begins with observation. He argued that no matter how many observations that you make, you cannot infer that your next observation will be identical. This is known as _____.

    a. deductive logic

    b. the problem of induction

    c. anomalous evidence

    d. trial and error

15. To help in summarizing numerical information, social scientists routinely rely on _____.

    a. scientific formulas

    b. the work of other scientists

    c. theoretical interpretation

    d. statistical techniques

Critical Thinking

1. This chapter introduces the very important notion of value-free or unbiased research. If our perceptions of reality can be affected by our values, then how can scientists ever be certain that what they see is true? Chapter 1 asked you to think about the suicide of Kurt Cobain. Now, imagine that you have been hired (and will be paid a lot of money) as a sociologist to investigate his death. Can you think of any personal biases or value judgments that might affect your method of inquiry? Would your taste in music influence the research design that you would use for your study? Can value-free or unbiased research exist when studying humans?

2. In this chapter, the author asks what counts as scientific evidence and uses the criminal justice system as an example. In the cases of Guy Paul Morin and David Milgaard, the judges, juries, and prosecutors had all weighed evidence that they believed demonstrated the guilt of these men. Circumstantial evidence, filtered by expectations and values, had led justice astray. Subjective judgments seriously compromised these men's lives. It was only through DNA testing, or scientific evidence, that these men were set free. Does the existence of DNA testing change your attitudes as they relate to capital punishment? Are you likely to support capital punishment if an offender's guilt can be scientifically proven? Has your view changed because of DNA testing?

3. Without a doubt, the age of technology is upon us. The use of self-administered questionnaires has become a popular way of conducting interviews. Many of you have grown up in a world full of computers and have relied on them for school, work, and pleasure. Try to answer this question honestly: Have you ever completed an online survey, but pretended to be someone

else? Have you ever used your pet's name or changed your age? What about submitting information to the online dating sites, or just checking out the people that do use these services? How much of the information that you see on the Internet is true? How reliable and valid do you think this information is?

4. Brian Wilson (2002) used a number of different methods to gather important information about the youth subculture in Canada. Not only did he become a participant observer by attending rave meetings and parties, he also interviewed people who were actually ravers. Do you think that the Hawthorne effect biased his study? If you were asked to research the same group of ravers, what would you do differently?

Web Links

Online Social Research Methods
http://www.ecommons.net/aoir/aoir2003/index.php?p=3
This website offers scholarly opinions concerning Online Social Research Methods. It's interesting to compare your feelings to the scientists that have actually studied the ethics of online research.

RJ's Research Methods
http://geography.ucsm.ac.uk/rj/links/RM_bkmk.html
Though not based in Canada, this website is an excellent resource for anyone new to social research. It provides all kinds of information about social research and also provides a wide variety of links that connect you to even more information in this area.

Methods, Statistics & the Research Paper
http://www.trinity.edu/~mkearl/methods.html
This is an excellent resource for anyone looking for more information about social research methods. It also offers help with writing research papers and provides a link to some common data banks.

Internet for Social Research Methods
http://www.vts.rdn.ac.uk/tutorial/social-research-methods
This site offers a free and really valuable tutorial that can assist you in developing your Internet information skills.

Solutions

True or False?

1. T

2. T

3. T

4. T

5. F

6. T

7. T

8. F

9. T

10. T

13. C

14. B

15. D

Multiple Choice

1. A

2. C

3. B

4. D

5. B

6. B

7. C

8. C

9. D

10. B

11. A

12. D

Chapter 3

Culture

Chapter Introduction

Stop for a moment and reflect on how you felt about living in Canada before you read this chapter and compare it with how you feel now. Have your feelings about your homeland changed in any way? Do you get a better sense of just how diverse our country is? I often wonder what it would be like to travel around the world, and have always been envious of those who do spend a lot of time travelling and experiencing new and exciting places. I don't know about you, but I've never had the "travel bug" and am quite content to stay right where I am. Reading this chapter allows you to visit a number of different cultures without having to leave the comfort of your own home and enlightens you on some of the more positive and negative consequences of living in a culturally diverse community. More than ever, Canadian students are travelling to China, Japan, and Korea to teach English as a second language to students of all ages. Practise your newly found critical thinking skills and imagine what your life would be like if you had to live in a foreign country for a year. How would you prepare yourself for the changes that you would face? What would be the determining factor in choosing a country — would the weather affect your decision more than the food? Would the politics of that nation require you to alter some of your current political beliefs? So many times we are faced with opportunities that challenge us in a variety of ways. Though these challenges often mean having to make important decisions, can you imagine living in a world without diversity? How very boring that would be.

This chapter should make you think about Canada from a number of different viewpoints and hopefully you'll see how cultural sharing takes place through social transmission. You'll soon learn that culture is the sum of the socially transmitted ideas, practices, and material objects that enable people to adapt to and thrive in their environments.

Learning Objectives

At the conclusion of this chapter, you should be able to discuss or write about the following, without having to rely on the textbook:

1. Humans have been able to adapt to their environments because they're able to create culture. Specifically, they can create symbols, cooperate with others, and make tools that enable them to thrive.

2. Culture can be invisible if we are too deeply immersed in it. The cultures of others can seem inscrutable if we view them exclusively from the perspective of our own culture. Therefore, the best vantage point for analyzing culture is on the margins, as it were — neither too deeply immersed in it nor too much removed from it.

3. Culture becomes more diversified and consensus declines in many areas of life as societies become more complex. This increases human freedom, giving people more choice in their ethnic, religious, sexual, and other identities.

4. So much cultural diversification and reconfiguration has taken place that some sociologists characterize the culture of our times as postmodern. Postmodernism involves an eclectic mixture

of cultural elements from different times and places, the erosion of authority, and the decline of consensus around core values.

5. While the diversification of culture increases human freedom, the growth of complex societies also establishes definite limits within which this diversification may occur. This is illustrated by the process of rationalization, the optimization of means to achieve a given end.

6. Although culture is created to solve human problems, it sometimes has negative consequences that create new problems. This is illustrated by the growth of consumerism, which as resulted in dangerously high levels of consumption.

7. The market (competition) is insufficient to solve the environmental problems that have resulted from our consumer society. In addition, increased cooperation is required.

Quiz Questions

True or False?

1. As societies become more complex, culture becomes more diversified and consensus declines in many areas of life. This decreases human freedom.
    True or False

2. Rewards and punishments aimed at ensuring conformity are known as sanctions of the system of social control.
    True or False

3. Culture is the sum of ideas, practices, and material objects that people create in order to adapt to and thrive in their world.
    True or False

4. Judging another culture exclusively by the standards of one's own is called ethnocentrism.
    True or False

5. Inexpensive international travel and communication make contacts between people from diverse cultures routine.
    True or False

6. Although culture is created to solve human problems, it sometimes has negative consequences that create new problems.
    True or False

7. The postmodern condition disempowers ordinary people, leaving them with little or no control over their own fate.
    True or False

8. As societies become more complex, the limits within which freedom may increase become more rigid, constraining human freedom.
    True or False

9. The English language is dominant because Britain and the United States have been the world's most powerful and influential countries — economically, militarily, and culturally for 200 years.
    True or False

10. The richest third of humanity earns about 80 times more than the poorest fifth (up from 30 times more in 1950).
    True or False

Multiple Choice

1. Globalization destroys _____ isolation, bringing people together in what Marshall McLuhan called a global village.
    a. political, economic, and cultural
    b. cultural, technological, and religious
    c. political, judicial, and religious
    d. cultural, political, and judicial

2. Which of the following is not true?
    a. Postmodernism involves an eclectic mixing of elements from different times and places.
    b. Postmodernism involves the erosion of authority.
    c. Postmodernism involves a heightened awareness of the masses.
    d. Postmodernism involves the decline of consensus about core values.

3. Which is not a tool in the human survival kit?
    a. abstraction
    b. cooperation
    c. production
    d. technology

4. Sociologists define _____ as all the ideas, practices, and material objects that people create to deal with real-life problems.
    a. culture
    b. society
    c. postmodernism
    d. subculture

5. Research shows that the average North American prefers to stand _____ inches away from strangers or acquaintances when they are engaged in face-to-face interaction.
    a. 20 to 26
    b. 30 to 36
    c. 40 to 46
    d. 50 to 56

6. Cultural freedom develops within definite limits. In particular, our lives are increasingly governed by the twin forces of _____.
    a. consumerism and rationalization
    b. consumerism and technology
    c. technology and rationalization
    d. none of the above

7. A_____ is a cultural ceremony that marks the transition from one stage of life to another or from life to death.
    a. ritual
    b. custom
    c. rite of passage
    d. tradition

8. Clocks, known as *Werkglocken*, were created in Germany and signified _____.
    a. the creation of unions
    b. the practice known as work to rule
    c. the beginning of the workday, the timing of meals, and quitting time
    d. the efficiency of assembly-line work

9. Rationalization is _____ term for the systematic application of the standardized means to predetermined ends.
    a. Schmanker's
    b. Marx's
    c. Durkheim's
    d. Weber's

10. The capacity to create ideas or ways of thinking is referred to as _____.
    a. production
    b. cooperation
    c. abstraction
    d. creativity

11. The tendency to define ourselves in terms of the goods we purchase is known as _____.
    a. Instant Gratification Syndrome
    b. consumerism
    c. competition
    d. Fashionism

12. As societies become more complex, culture becomes more diversified and consensus declines in many areas of life. This also increases _____.
    a. our ability to become better consumers
    b. our human freedom
    c. divisions among the classes that exist in society
    d. our awareness of other cultures

13. Allowing clocks to regulate our activities precisely seems the most natural thing in the world and is a pretty good sign that the internalized *Werkglock* is, in fact, a product of _____.
    a. capitalism
    b. culture
    c. technology
    d. changing times

14. _____ is the godfather of heavy metal. Beginning in the 1960s, he and his band, Black Sabbath, inspired Metallica, Kiss, Judas Priest, Marilyn Manson, and others to play loud, nihilistic music, reject conventional morality, embrace death and violence, and foment youthful rebellion and parental panic.

    a. Tommy Lee

    b. Perry Como

    c. Glen Campbell

    d. Ozzy Ozbourne

15. Hockey legend Wayne Gretzky would tuck only the right side of his jersey into his pants. This superstitious practice helped to put his mind at ease before and during play. It is an example of how people create _____ to cope with anxiety and other concrete problems they face.

    a. culture

    b. safety nets

    c. personal anomalies

    d. routines

Critical Thinking

1. Do you think there is any foundation for superstitious beliefs? If not, how can you explain the fact that so many people are superstitious? Do you have any superstitions? Have you ever broken a superstition — walked under a ladder or broken a mirror? If so, what were the results?

2. Have you ever lived in another culture? If so how does your own culture differ from the one you lived in or visited? If you haven't lived in another culture, you likely know someone who comes from another country. Have you learned about their customs and beliefs? To what degree does ethnocentrism affect how and what you think of that person?

3. Can you imagine buying a Big Mac from a vending machine? Have you ever had a job at a fast-food restaurant? In this chapter, Ritzer paints a fairly bleak picture of these jobs and ways of buying food. Is it really as bad as he makes it seem? If it is, what accounts for the fact that teenagers work in most fast-food restaurants? What are other employment opportunities for teens?

4. "It's not the steak we sell. It's the sizzle." This statement was made about advertising in the 1940s. How much does advertising really influence us? At what age do you think advertising starts to influence us? Do we ever become aware of its influences? Have you bought or boycotted a product just because of the advertising? Are you likely to do so, and under what circumstances?

Web Links

Yahoo! Directory Society and Culture
http://dir.yahoo.com/Society_and_Culture/
This website is standard Yahoo fare and offers you the opportunity to discover a great deal of information on different kinds of cultures from cowboy cultures to drug cultures — the possibilities here are endless. A great site to find ideas for a term paper.

World Diversity
http://www.diversityworld.com/
This website offers information on training and educating a variety of diverse workers to reduce employment barriers.

Smithsonian Institution
http://www.si.edu/
This is simply an amazing website. The Smithsonian Institution offers an incredible abundance of information from cultures around the world. Time spent learning from this site is definitely worthwhile.

Culture Online — Amercian Sociological Association Section on the Sociology of Culture
http://www.ncf.edu/culture/
This website offers cultural information from a sociological viewpoint. It's very scholarly, but gives you an idea of what it would be like to write publishable papers on a different culture.

Solutions

True or False?

1. F
2. T
3. T
4. T
5. T
6. T
7. F
8. T
9. T
10. F

Multiple Choice

1. A
2. C
3. D
4. A
5. B
6. A
7. C
8. C
9. D
10. C
11. B
12. B
13. A
14. D
15. A

Chapter 4

Socialization

Chapter Introduction

When does socialization begin and when does it end? Is it something that we have control over or something that occurs without conscious thought? Can we become better people through socialization? Answers to these questions have invariably remained the same over time, and I think that it's because we take the process of socialization for granted. We don't often think of changing the way we've been socialized because we're really not aware that it has happened until after the fact.

This chapter explains that socialization is a lifelong process that begins when you're born and doesn't end until your life is over. However, I often argue that the process of socialization begins even before you're born. Think of the friends or family that you know that have had children. What are the preconceived notions that people have about newborn babies? What colour will the nursery be if it's a girl? What if it's a boy? Although these gender stereotypes are not as prevalent as they used to be, I think that even before they're born, babies have started the socialization process.

Socialization is all about the relationships and circumstances that you use to explore who you are and what you are about. Sociologists and psychologists agree that your self-image really depends a lot on social interaction. Since we spend the majority of our formative years with relatives, the family is the most important agent of socialization. As a general rule, our family members have more influence over our lives than our friends and peers even though it may not seem like it. Other agents of socialization include the media and religion, but the degree to which these institutions affect the definition of our social selves is largely an individual determination. I tend to think that I can't be swayed toward the purchase of a certain product simply by its advertising campaigns, but then there are other times when I know that I buy certain things based solely on their advertising. I often followed the advice of my peers rather than the advice of my parents. Though we are solely responsible for defining who we are, we ultimately make this decision through interacting with others.

This chapter takes the approach that socialization is an active process, one in which those being socialized participate in and contribute to that socialization. The authors also point out that it's an interactive process in which those who are socializing are undergoing a learning process themselves. What I think that you'll learn is that the most important learning, the crucial learning that transforms us into cultural beings, proceeds through interaction with others who are important to us and, usually, to whom we are also important.

Learning Objectives

At the conclusion of this chapter, you should be able to discuss or write about the following, without having to rely on the textbook:

1. Socialization is an active process through which human beings become members of society, develop a sense of self, and learn to participate in social relationships with others.

2. Through socialization we acquire the knowledge, skills, and motivations that we need to participate in society.

3. Socialization is a lifelong process.

4. Charles Horton Cooley is best known for his concept of the "looking-glass self," which stressed that we view ourselves as we think others view us. George Herbert Mead emphasized how people assume roles by imagining themselves in the roles of others. Erving Goffman described the intricate ways that we try to present ourselves when interacting with others.

5. Though there are many agents of socialization (peers, media), the most important agent of socialization is the family.

6. Schools expose children to situations in which the same rules, regulations, and authority patterns apply to everyone.

7. During adulthood, individuals are socialized into a number of different roles as they get married, find a career, retire, and eventually die. All of these roles involve new and different relationships with others and also act as guidelines for behaviour.

8. Resocialization occurs when we abandon or are forced to abandon our way of life and self-concept for a radically different one. Usually, this is done in total institutions, for example, prisons or boot camps.

Quiz Questions

True or False?

1. Sociologists are suspicious of explanations that emphasize biological inheritance because such explanations often shift from an initial focus on individual differences to an emphasis on group differences.
    True or False

2. Sociologists and psychologists both agree that even though we are influenced by others, our self-image is a creation based solely on inner reflection.
    True or False

3. Taking the role of the other is an essential skill that a child must develop to be an effective member of society.
    True or False

4. George Herbert Mead's dramaturgical approach uses the analogy of life as theatre and of people as actors putting on performances for one another.
    True or False

5. Socialization can be a matter of life and death.
    True or False

6. The peer group is the only agent of childhood socialization over which adults have little control.
    True or False

7. Studies show that gender stereotyping has decreased but is still prevalent in children's literature.
    True or False

8. A peer group is a set of individuals who are about the same age, share similar interests, and enjoy a similar social status.
    True or False

9. The consensus among sociologists is that violence in the mass media may push some people to engage in more violent acts.
    True or False

10. Becoming parents accentuates gender roles and the sexual division of labour in heterosexual couples.
    True or False

Multiple Choice

1. Mead used the term _____ to refer to the widespread and shared set of cultural norms and values used in self-evaluation and developing concepts of the self.
    a. taking the role of the other
    b. the generalized other
    c. the looking-glass self
    d. self-fulfilling prophecy

2. _____ is the process by which adults take on new statuses and acquire new and different social identities.
    a. Socialization
    b. Adult socialization
    c. Anticipatory socialization
    d. Primary socialization

3. The self, for Cooley, has three major elements. Which of the following is not one of them?
    a. how we think our physical appearance is seen by another person
    b. our perception of other people's judgments about us
    c. our actual appearance
    d. our reaction to how we believe others judge us

4. _____ uses the individual rather than the group as the frame of reference; emphasis is placed on the development of the person.
    a. Ethnomethodology
    b. Symbolic interactionism
    c. Structural functionalism
    d. Radical theorism

5. A _____ is a group of people within the larger culture that has distinctive values, norms, and practices.
    a. sect
    b. counterculture
    c. cult
    d. subculture

6. Rosenthal and Jacobson (1968) demonstrated the power of _____ — when an expectation leads to behaviour that causes the expectation to become a reality.

   a. the looking-glass self

   b. intrinsic predetermination

   c. the self-fulfilling prophecy

   d. subconscious thinking

7. Adolescence as a distinct period of life is a product of _____.

   a. socialization

   b. dual-parent employment

   c. industrialization

   d. war

8. Which of the following is not a characteristic of Freud's theory?

   a. gender

   b. id

   c. superego

   d. ego

9. When we share in both the larger society and in a specific part of it, we are influenced by distinctive _____ of family, friends, class, and religion.

   a. primary groups

   b. peer groups

   c. subcultures

   d. relations

10. Which of the following describes groups of people usually of a similar age and equal social status?

    a. cohorts

    b. subcultures

    c. peer groups

    d. formal groups

11. Within _____ of childbirth, first-time parents saw daughters as softer, finer featured, and more delicate than sons.

    a. two days

    b. one day

    c. a few hours

    d. an hour

12. Conversion is often an example of _____, the process of discarding former patterns of behaviour and belief and accepting new ones, although at times, reluctantly.

    a. resocialization

    b. anticipatory socialization

    c. brainwashing

    d. primary socialization

13. For most Canadians, mandatory retirement from the labour force occurs at age _____.

    a. 55

    b. 60

    c. 65

    d. 70

14. Of all the functions of _____, adjusting children to a social order — which offers a preview of what will be expected of them as they negotiate their way to adulthood — may be the most important.

    a. a peer group

    b. the family

    c. the media

    d. education

15. It is during _____ that most dramatic transformations of identity, status, and social relationships tend to occur.

    a. infancy

    b. childhood

    c. adolescence

    d. adulthood

Critical Thinking

1. The nature vs. nurture debate has been around for many years, but is still controversial. As we try to understand social change, we often fall back to this age old argument. Does nature play a bigger role than the environment in determining who we are, or is it the other way around? What do you think? Use this argument to discuss intelligence and then use it to discuss alcoholism — do your answers differ?

2. The self-fulfilling prophecy is a frequently debated topic in sociology, and Rosenthal and Jacobson's IQ study serves as a landmark case in the study of socialization. They conducted their research in 1968. Do you consider this study to be ethical? Do you think that you could replicate this study today? If so, what changes would you make to the methodology of this work?

3. To be socialized means to learn how to act and interact appropriately with others and to transform oneself into a member of society. To be socialized is also to develop a self, a sense of individual identity that allows us to understand ourselves and differentiate ourselves from others. When did you first discover your "self"? Does the true you fit into most social situations or do you find yourself acting a lot of the time? Does your "self" change very often? If so, when does it change and why? Do you often find yourself trying to impress someone by hiding your true self and pretending that you're something that you're not?

4. The chapter discusses extreme ends of the academic setting when it presents information on kindergarten boot camps and home schooling. What are the advantages and disadvantages of each school? Would the socialization of school children be affected by these surroundings? If so, how would the socialization process differ? What are your thoughts on each of these forms of learning? Would you enroll your children in either of these "schools"?

Web Links

ASA on Socialization
http://www2.pfeiffer.edu/~lridener/DSS/socialization.htm
The American Sociological Association's web page on socialization offers a wide range of information on a variety of issues that are addressed by socialization factors. Learn more about the social processes that children go through or read more about Cooley's "looking-glass self" theory.

CanTeach: Links — Homeschooling
http://www.canteach.ca/links/linkhomeschool.html
This is a great site to learn more about homeschooling It provides information on the advantages and disadvantages of homeschooling and other related topics.

A History of Education
http://fcis.oise.utoronto.ca/~daniel_schugurensky/assignment1/index.html
This is a site about education during the 20th century, organized by decades. It includes a short description of a variety of educational episodes that took place in that period.

Basic Correctional Treatment and Resocialization
http://www.tyc.state.tx.us/programs/basic_treat.html
This American website offers an interesting look at the concept of resocialization as it occurs in the United States.

Solutions

13. C

14. D

15. C

True or False?

1. T

2. F

3. T

4. F

5. T

6. T

7. T

8. T

9. F

10. T

Multiple Choice

1. B

2. B

3. C

4. B

5. D

6. C

7. C

8. A

9. C

10. C

11. B

12. A

Chapter 5

Sex, Gender, and Sexuality

Chapter Introduction

In today's society men, women, and children are becoming more and more aware of their sexuality and the sexuality of others. Dr. Ruth and Sue Johanson have brought the topic of sex out of the closet and into the living rooms of millions of people. I taught a course in human sexuality this past term and I was totally amazed at how sexually explicit my students were. It would seem as though the topic of sex is not to be whispered in hushed tones as it once was. I blushed more than once at their openness, but at the same time, was so very proud of them for speaking up about their feelings. The story of David Reimer acts as an incredible reminder of the importance of enjoying a quality of life that meets our own expectations. Is living inside a shell that masks our inner beings really living? How can we enjoy each day knowing that there are precious moments of our lives that we're not living to the fullest? Sexual acceptance and tolerance of others are such incredibly important concepts to both understand and practise. As our world grows more and more culturally diverse, it also expands its boundaries in terms of social and sexual acceptance for all — not just those who fit the skin that they're born in, but also those who struggle to get out.

This chapter asks how we define what is male and what is female and investigates the relationship between biological sex and the attitudes and behaviours that we associate with being male or female. What are the implications of this relationship for our sexual identity and sexual relationships? While introducing you to the concepts of sex and gender, this chapter also offers a wealth of sociological and psychological evidence that explains how the interpretation of these two terms can affect your life and the lives of others.

Learning Objectives

At the conclusion of this chapter, you should be able to discuss or write about the following, without having to rely on the textbook:

1. Sex refers to biological differences between males and females, while gender refers to the attitudes, beliefs, and behaviours that we commonly associate with each sex.

2. Though it's popular to trace the origins of masculine and feminine gender roles to biological differences, there are many ways in which gender is socially constructed.

3. Three major historical changes have led to the development of gender inequality: long-distance warfare and conquest, plough agriculture, and the separation of public and private spheres during early industrialization

4. Conscious sexual learning begins around adolescence and occurs within the context of firmly established gender identities.

5. Sexual relationships tend to be male-dominated as a result of gender socialization and men's continuing dominant position in society.

6. The social construction of gender and sexual scripts has defined standards of beauty that are nearly impossible for most women to achieve. This contributes to widespread anxiety about body image and, in some cases, leads to eating disorders.

7. Gender inequality and a social context that justifies sexual aggression in men contribute to the widespread problem of male sexual aggression.

8. The mass media reflect and reinforce the relationship between heterosexuality and male domination.

Quiz Questions

True or False?

1. Your gender depends on whether you were born with distinct male or female genitalia and a genetic program that released either male or female hormones to stimulate the development of your reproductive system.
   True or False

2. Transgendered people are individuals who want to alter their gender by changing their appearance or resorting to medical intervention.
   True or False

3. Sociobiologists are concerned with male–female differences in sexual scripts, the division of labour at home and in the workplace, mate selection, sexual aggression, and so forth.
   True or False

4. Sexual pluralists believe that pornography does not have to reinforce the domination and degradation of women by men but it can allow women to create their own sexual fantasies.
   True or False

5. Premarital sex is widely accepted by the Canadian public.
   True or False

6. Essentialists argue that gender differences are not the product of biological properties, whether chromosomal, gonadal, or hormonal. Instead, gender and sexuality are products of social structure and culture.
   True or False

7. Research demonstrates that, in general, victims of sexual assault are selected less because of sexual desirability than because of their availability and powerlessness.
   True or False

8. Quid pro quo sexual harassment involves sexual jokes, comments, and touching that interferes with work or creates an unfriendly work setting.
   True or False

9. North Americans' expectations about how men and women are supposed to act have not changed much over the last 40 years.
   True or False

10. In our society, there is little formal socialization — that is, systematic instruction — regarding sexuality.
    True or False

Multiple Choice

1. Evidence suggests that if gender reassignment takes place before the age of _____ months, it tends to be successful.
    a. 12
    b. 18
    c. 24
    d. 36

2. A 1997 survey shows that _____ percent of North American women want to lose weight.
    a. 22
    b. 56
    c. 77
    d. 89

3. At the point of conception, a newly formed zygote has _____ chromosomes. If the last chromosome has an XX pattern, the zygote becomes a female.
    a. 24
    b. 36
    c. 46
    d. 48

4. _____ people are individuals who want to alter their gender by changing their appearance or resorting to medical intervention.
    a. Asexual
    b. Transvestic
    c. Hermaphroditic
    d. Transgendered

5. Differences between the sex organs are noticeable by the _____ week after conception.
    a. fifth
    b. fourteenth
    c. twentieth
    d. thirty-second

6. One's identification with, or sense of belonging to, a particular sex — biologically, psychologically, and socially — is known as one's _____.
    a. gender identity
    b. gender
    c. sex
    d. sexual orientation

31

7. In the agricultural era, economic production was organized around the _____.

    a. household

    b. father's income

    c. factory

    d. skills of artisans

8. Sociobiology is the best-known variant of essentialism and _____ is its leading exponent.

    a. Charles Darwin

    b. Mark Granovetter

    c. E. O. Wilson

    d. Max Weber

9. By the age of about _____, interaction with peers becomes an important factor in reinforcing gender-typed attitudes and behaviours.

    a. 4

    b. 8

    c. 10

    d. 14

10. Homosexuality was considered a serious psychiatric disorder from the early 1880s until _____, when it was finally dropped from the *Diagnostic and Statistical Manual of Mental Disorders*, the standard diagnostic tool used by North American psychiatrists.

    a. 1965

    b. 1974

    c. 1980

    d. 1985

11. Sociologist Reginald Bibby predicts that by about 2010, only a durable core of some 15 percent of the population will continue to be opposed to _____.

    a. cohabitation

    b. premarital sex

    c. homosexuality

    d. transsexuality

12. Social constructionists stress three main sociological changes that led to the development of gender inequality. Which of the following is not one of them?

    a. long-distance warfare and conquest

    b. the suffragette movement

    c. plough agriculture

    d. the separation of public and private spheres

13. A 2001 survey of 18 500 16- to 55-year-olds provides recent information on sexual behaviour in 28 countries and concludes that _____ have sexual intercourse most often — 124 times per year, on average.

    a. Greeks

    b. Canadians

    c. Spaniards

    d. Americans

14. Which of the following is not a critique of the essentialist theory?

    a. Essentialists ignore the historical and cultural variability of gender and sexuality.

    b. The research evidence employed by essentialists is often flawed.

    c. Essentialists fail to consider the demographic shifts that occur over time.

    d. Essentialists ignore the fact that gender differences are declining rapidly.

15. Even today, many people assume that individuals should desire only members of the opposite sex. Sociologists call this assumption _____.

    a. discrimination

    b. compulsory heterosexuality

    c. homophobia

    d. predetermined gender assumptions

Critical Thinking

1. The story of David Reimer is an incredible journey of courage and determination that puts forth a number of questions concerning the notions of sex and sexuality. In your opinion, should men and women that suffer from gender ambiguity be assisted in their struggle to find the right fit? As a society, how much assistance should we offer? For example, should the costs of counselling and surgery be covered by a provincial health insurance plan? Why or why not?

2. The findings of many research studies conducted to learn more about homosexuality often depend heavily on how homosexuality is measured. If you were a social researcher investigating the prevalence of homosexuality in high school students, how would you define the term "homosexuality"? How would you measure it? For example, if an individual has had same-sex fantasies but has not had a same-sex relationship, would you consider that person to be homosexual? Would your definition of homosexuality differ if your sample was comprised of graduate students?

3. Surveys are a popular method that provide evidence of a wide variation in attitudes towards sex or sexuality and, consequently, help to dispel the myths that surround these concepts. Since much of the information gathered by surveys relies on self-reporting, how reliable and valid is the information that we get from them? How honest are people likely to be when reporting information on such an intimate part of their lives? How reliable and valid is the data obtained from these sources?

4. According to the chapter, in most schools teachers still tend to assume that boys will do better in the sciences and mathematics and that girls will excel in languages. It also says that parents reinforce these expectations at home. Do you agree or disagree with these statements? Were you "guided" into a gender-appropriate stream when you were in high school? How can you stop the perpetuation of these gender-biased stereotypes?

Web Links

From Sex to Humanity: How to be Human — A Guide in Two Parts (Part 1)
http://www.firstscience.com/SITE/ARTICLES/human.asp
This website contains an article written by Peter Moore and provides an unbiased view on sexuality and the role that appearance plays in defining it.

Open Directory — Society: Sexuality
http://dmoz.org/Society/Sexuality/
Included is an extensive listing of concepts and definitions that deal with sex and gender.

An Evolutionary Hypothesis for Eating Disorders
http://cogprints.ecs.soton.ac.uk/archive/00000800/00/eatdis~1.htm
This site offers an excellent sociological study of eating disorders.

Gender Bias in Education
http://www.edchange.org/multicultural/papers/genderbias.html
Written by a college student, this essay is a good example of gender bias in society and is a relatively easy read.

Solutions

True or False?

1. F
2. T
3. F
4. T
5. T
6. F
7. T
8. F
9. T
10. T

Multiple Choice

1. B
2. D
3. C
4. D
5. B
6. A
7. A
8. C
9. D
10. B
11. B
12. B
13. D
14. C
15. B

Chapter 6

The Mass Media

Chapter Introduction

Can you imagine having to live your life without a computer, or without the luxury of watching television each night before you go to bed? Without a doubt, the media have a staggering effect on our lives, regardless of how often we watch television or read the daily news. It is virtually impossible to exist in most places without having access to some form of media — television, radio, newspapers, magazines, and billboards are all types of media that keep us informed on what's happening and what's not happening — often when we really don't care about either. As an instructor and a student still working on my doctorate, I find that I don't have the time to be aware of much of what goes on in the world. Oddly enough, this doesn't affect my ability to carry on meaningful conversations with both students and colleagues and, in all honesty, I could easily live without a television. I couldn't live without a computer and I would give up food before I gave up books. If you had to relinquish one or the other for a month, which would it be? How much would it change your life? Are you easily duped into buying items that you really don't need because you like the product's advertising campaign? Though I try not too, I sometimes fall prey to impulsive shopping and buy things based solely on the commercials that advertise them.

This chapter explores the different forms of media that affect our lives and offers a variety of theoretical viewpoints that help us understand the media as an important influence in our society. By addressing four main ideas that surround the media, the author gives some very clear ideas concerning political economy, representation and ideology, media effects and audiences, and the Internet.

Learning Objectives

At the conclusion of this chapter, you should be able to discuss or write about the following, without having to rely on the textbook:

1. Canadian newspapers have high levels of ownership concentration, are usually part of larger multimedia chains, and function largely as local monopolies. The factor that has the greatest impact on news content, however, is the dependency on advertising.

2. In the case of television, advertising dependency, the high costs of production, and audience preferences mean that much of the programming Canadians watch is foreign — primarily American.

3. Conservatives claim that news coverage has a left-liberal political bias that is unrepresentative of society's mainstream. Critical theorists argue that news coverage is ideologically conservative, in that it defines reality from a perspective of dominant ideology and views events and issues through the lens of social control.

4. The majority of observers believe that there is a causal link between television and violent behaviour, but the studies that support this view have been criticized on the grounds of flawed methodology. Further, the majority view is split on the issue of how television causes aggression.

Some argue that watching TV counteracts the effects of socialization by weakening self-control; others believe that it, in fact, socializes children in the use of violence.

5. Studies of audiences indicate that TV viewing and the responses to it vary according to gender. Men are more likely to watch attentively and privately, whereas women watch in a more interactive, social way. Women also tend to be more open about their TV viewing and use TV as a topic of casual social interaction and conversation.

6. While early views about the development of computer-mediated communication and the Internet tended to polarize between optimists and pessimists, recent research has yielded a more complex, balanced view.

7. Research on the impact of the Internet shows that virtual communities develop normative structures like real communities, and function as sources of identity and social solidarity. For the most part, however, life online supplements and complements real-world social interaction and involvement rather than replacing it.

Quiz Questions

True or False?

1. Despite the decline in television viewing, research indicates that we spend more time interacting with the media than doing anything else, including working.
    True or False

2. Space-biased media are modes of communication that endure over time but are not very mobile across space, such as writing on stone or clay tablets.
    True or False

3. Political economy focuses on the ownership and control of economic resources, and on the effect of technology and economic power on cultural values, social structure, and political decision-making.
    True or False

4. The world's dominant media corporations are primarily American-based.
    True or False

5. Desensitization refers to the possibility that continued exposure to violent imagery may weaken the mechanisms of self-control that an individual acquires through socialization and that discourage the use of violence.
    True or False

6. One of the main arguments of the cultivation perspective is that people who watch a lot of television, and are exposed to more TV violence, perceive society to be more violent and dangerous than it really is. Gerbner and colleagues call this the "mean world" syndrome.
    True or False

7. Virtual communities resemble real communities inasmuch as they entail not only shared values and a sense of belonging but also a common project or purpose.
    True or False

8. Television dramas generally reproduce gender stratification in occupational roles. Women are more likely to be seen as office workers and in family settings.
    True or False

9. Horizontal integration refers to the controlling of resources and assets at the different stages of production, such as ownership of a major league sports team along with the stations and cable channels over which the games are televised.
    True or False

10. Early research and commentary on the Internet tended to polarize between optimists who saw CMC positively (as a vehicle for greater democracy, globalism, and identity experimentation) and those critics who focus on such negative effects as disengagement from "real" social relations and the spread of offensive images and ideas like pornography and racism.
    True or False

Multiple Choice

1. Access to and use of the Internet reflects broader patterns of _____, though these may decline as the use of technology becomes less costly.

    a. educational attainment

    b. gender inequality

    c. social inequality

    d. regional dependence

2. The most commonly used form of CMC among Canadians is _____.

    a. e-mail

    b. general browsing

    c. formal education/training

    d. purchasing goods and services

3. When the media focuses on certain issues while playing down or ignoring others, the process is called_____.

    a. framing

    b. selective representation

    c. biased reporting

    d. priming

4. According to the _____ perspective, institutions such as the media and processes such as socialization and social control cannot be understood from the viewpoint of society as a whole, but only from that of unequal and conflicting groups and classes.

    a. structural functionalist

    b. critical

    c. symbolic interaction

    d. essentialist

5. The average Canadian spends about _____ hours a week watching television.

   a. 8.5

   b. 17.5

   c. 21.5

   d. 30

6. In the realm of MUDs, newsgroups, and chat rooms, lurking can act as a form of _____ by allowing newbies to familiarize themselves with the group's practices and language codes before becoming active posters.

   a. primary socialization

   b. anticipatory socialization

   c. secondary socialization

   d. resocialization

7. News sources that do not have an organizational or group affiliation but are usually eyewitnesses or victims of newsworthy events and issues are called _____.

   a. ordinary news sources

   b. alternative news sources

   c. unreliable news sources

   d. independent news sources

8. Only _____ of the top ten media corporations are based outside the United States.

   a. 2

   b. 3

   c. 4

   d. 5

9. News _____ tends to focus on the activities of certain social actors rather than others, so it also tends to rely on and privilege certain sources of information over others.

   a. streaming

   b. marking

   c. censuring

   d. framing

10. Edward Herman and Noam Chomsky argue that the media serve the interests of the political and economic elites by _____ information to reduce or eliminate radical or subversive views.

   a. framing

   b. filtering

   c. suppressing

   d. ignoring

11. As of 2002, about _____ of the world's population are online.
    a. 1%
    b. 3%
    c. 8%
    d. 10%

12. Which of the following is not considered to be one of the three major criteria used to determine newsworthiness?
    a. sensationalism
    b. immediacy
    c. personalization
    d. extraordinariness

13. _____ refers to a situation in which one society's media exert an overwhelming and unilateral influence over another society's culture.
    a. Cultural domination
    b. Cultural hinterland
    c. Cultural hierarchy
    d. Cultural imperialism

14. Studies of the effects of television on behaviour have been subject to a variety of criticisms ranging from ideological bias to imprecise concepts to a misplaced focus on individual psychology at the expense of social processes. The most significant criticisms, however, have been _____.
    a. methodological
    b. theoretical
    c. analytical
    d. logical

15. Initial access to the Internet is typically marked by a strong gender bias and is particularly evident in Canada and _____, where women now (slightly) outnumber men online.
    a. Japan
    b. Germany
    c. France
    d. the United States

Critical Thinking

1. Ownership and control of the media are generally becoming more concentrated into a smaller number of larger corporate hands. Are you aware of the relationship that exists between the media and big business? As a consumer of a variety of media forms, how does this relationship affect you? For example, how does network ownership affect the news? The textbook example of CanWest Global and the *Ottawa Citizen* should offer some insight on this question.

2. Researchers have found that the introduction of TV has led to the displacement of other activities that have a social element attached to them. Has the availability of stay-at-home shopping, banking, working, and entertainment diminished the time that you would normally spend doing these things in person? Can you imagine a time when you won't ever have to leave your home? Would you find other ways to socialize or would you be content just staying indoors?

3. Television is a heterogeneous medium and its imagery is usually open to some interpretive variation. The degree of variation depends partly on the modality of the image — that is, the extent to which it approximates real life. Has the increase in reality TV that features real-life programs like *Survivor* and *The Osbournes* changed your views on what you think is real and what you think is fiction, as depicted by television? Is your family anything like the Osbournes? Would you want it to be?

4. Those who accept the majority view claim that there is consistent evidence for a link between television and real-life violence or aggressiveness, though the strength of the evidence varies according to the methodology. If you had the chance to research the relationship between television and aggression in children, how would you define and measure the concept of violence? Would your definitions and measurements differ if your sample was comprised of adults instead of children?

Web Links

ACCURACY IN MEDIA — For Fairness, Balance and Accuracy in News Reporting
http://www.aim.org/
Accuracy In Media is a non-profit, grassroots citizens watchdog of the news media that critiques botched and bungled news stories and sets the record straight on important issues that have received slanted coverage.

Media Watch: Media Literacy Through Education & Action
http://www.mediawatch.com/
Media Watch, which began in 1984, distributes educational videos, media literacy information, and newsletters to help create more informed consumers of the mass media.

Media and Society
http://www.ryerson.ca/mgroup/rlist.html
A collection of bibliographical information gathered from a number of sources and categorized by media form.

Media Awareness Network
http://www.media-awareness.ca/english/index.cfm
Resources and support for everyone interested in media and information literacy for young people.

Solutions

True or False?

1. T
2. F
3. T
4. T
5. F
6. T
7. T
8. T
9. F
10. T

Multiple Choice

1. C
2. A
3. D
4. B
5. C
6. B
7. A
8. B
9. D
10. B
11. C
12. A
13. D
14. A
15. D

Chapter 7

Religion

Chapter Introduction

In today's society, when it seems as though every day brings a new story of heartbreak and devastation somewhere in the world, where do you go to find solace among the sadness? For many people, in different ways, religion is the pathway through which they find peace and comfort. Is this the case with you?

When you take the time to reflect on some of the harder times in your life, what do you think helped you the most in getting through them? How much time, if any, do you spend wondering about what happens when you die? The answers to these questions have kept world thinkers and philosophers busy for centuries, and I suspect that they'll be just as busy for years to come. Regardless of how you measure or determine your level of religiosity, I hope that you have some way or some one to help you through the tougher times in life. Most people say that life is too short, but I'm a pessimist and I always counter them by saying that life is too long — to be doing things that don't make you happy.

This chapter examines what some of the early social scientists had to say about religion and explains the ways in which sociologists today study and bring meaning to this important institution at the individual and organized levels. By looking at how various researchers define religion and how they go about studying it, this chapter will give you a bird's eye view of religiosity in Canada and around the world. As you read through this chapter, try to think about your own religious habits and compare them to the practices of your parents and friends. What are some of the things that influence your religious beliefs and how do your beliefs influence others in society?

Learning Objectives

At the conclusion of this chapter, you should be able to discuss or write about the following, without having to rely on the textbook:

1. Sociology uses the scientific method to study religion, in contrast to religion, which explores reality beyond what can be known empirically.

2. The sociology of religion has been strongly influenced by the theoretical contributions of Marx, Durkheim, and Weber.

3. Religion can be defined as a system of meaning that uses the supernatural to interpret the world.

4. Personal religious commitment can be seen as having four dimensions: belief, practice, experience, and knowledge. Personal commitment is created and sustained by collective religiosity.

5. In Canada, organized religion has experienced a considerable decline in participation in recent years.

6. Reflection, socialization, and deprivation are used to explain religion at the individual level, and the secularization thesis is used to offer insight at the structural level.

7. Although religion can be socially disruptive, it more commonly seems to contribute to social solidarity.

8. Internationally, there is growing support for the persistence thesis.

9. The search for alleged religious drop-outs in Canada reveals that most people still identify with established religious groups.

10. The discrepancy between widespread belief and practices existing at the same time as relatively low commitment suggests that many people in Canada find it useful to draw selectively on religion, rather than embracing it as an all-encompassing system of meaning.

11. Religion's future will depend not only on social and individual needs, but also on the extent to which religious groups are effective as organizations in responding to widespread interest and need among people of all ages.

Quiz Questions

True or False?

1. The Protestant ethic is the sixteenth- and seventeenth-century Protestant belief that religious doubts can be reduced and a state of grace assured if people work diligently and live ascetically. According to Durkheim, the Protestant work ethic had the unintended effect of increasing savings and investments and thus stimulating capitalist growth.
   True or False

2. According to Marx, those who hold power encourage religious belief among the masses as a subtle tool for economic exploitation.
   True or False

3. Research shows that people who follow a religious/spiritual path are more likely to enjoy greater longevity and superior overall health than those who do not. Additionally, prayer, meditation, and other mind-body approaches, whether from the Eastern or Western religious models, appear to be beneficial to the healing process.
   True or False

4. Because they don't like to be seen as "big businesses" to their parishioners, churches frown on the practice of actually competing for members.
   True or False

5. Durkheim believed that besides meeting needs at the individual level, religion creates and reinforces social solidarity.
   True or False

6. In his classic work *The Elementary Forms of the Religious Life*, Weber argued that religion's origin is social. People who live in community come to share common sentiments, and as a result, a collective conscience is formed.
   True or False

7. Religion has been present in virtually every society and in sociological terms, religious organizations are no different from other social organizations.
   True or False

8. Science limits itself to what is perceivable and religion maintains that reality includes the non-perceivable.
    True or False

9. Stark and Glock (1968) suggested that the religions of the world typically expect their most devoted followers to hold key beliefs, engage in certain practices, have supernatural experiences, and be aware of the central tenets of their faith. They refer to these belief, practice, experience, and knowledge components of commitment as dimensions of religiosity.
    True or False

10. Auguste Comte worked from the assumption that religion is a human creation. He maintained, however, that it plays an important role in compensating people who are economically deprived.
    True or False

Multiple Choice

1. The ideas that we hold tend to come from our interaction with other people. _____ would maintain that personal religiosity is highly dependent on collective religiosity and group support of some kind.
    a. Marx
    b. Durkheim
    c. Weber
    d. none of the above

2. Census data show that when two parents have the same faith, _____ of their children are also raised in that faith.
    a. 65%
    b. 75%
    c. 85%
    d. 95%

3. _____ believed that religious beliefs articulate the nature of the sacred and its symbols, and religious rites provide guidelines as to how people should act in the presence of the sacred.
    a. Durkheim
    b. Marx
    c. Weber
    d. Freud

4. Weber noted that different groups in society vary in their inclination to be religious. Which of the following is not true?
    a. Women are much more religious than men.
    b. Peasants are religious when they are threatened.
    c. The nobility find religion beneath their honour.
    d. The working class supplants religion with other ideologies.

5. Surveys have found that Canadians exhibit relatively high levels of religious belief, practice, experience, and knowledge. Stark and Glock (1968) refer to the combination of these as _____.

    a. definitions of religiosity
    b. dimensions of religiosity
    c. requirements of religiosity
    d. the basis of religiosity

6. According to the 2000 Project Canada survey, only _____ of Canadians say that religion is "very important" to them, with most having fairly conventional ideas of religion in mind.

    a. 10%
    b. 13%
    c. 17%
    d. 21%

7. According to the 1991 census, _____ percent of Canadians indicated they had no religious preference.

    a. 5
    b. 8
    c. 13
    d. 17

8. Fewer than 5% of Canadians say that they regularly watch religious services on TV, and eight out of ten regular TV viewers also attend services weekly, but at least_____ of Canadians do not claim to be religiously committed, privately or otherwise.

    a. 30%
    b. 50%
    c. 60%
    d. 70%

9. Conrad Kanagy and Leo Driedger recently found that among _____ —a group widely stereotyped as resistant to change — there have been noteworthy changes in attitudes toward women, political participation, and pacifism since the early 1970s.

    a. Amish
    b. Quakers
    c. Shakers
    d. Mennonites

10. It is important to keep in mind that _____ appears to be a necessary but not a sufficient cause of religiosity.

    a. church attendance
    b. daily prayer ritual
    c. socialization
    d. parental influence

11. Proponents of the secularization thesis maintain that religion is bound to be replaced by science and reason. Karel Dobbelaere argues that this process has three aspects. Which of the following is not one of them?

    a. institutional

    b. cultural

    c. organizational

    d. personal

12. Which of the following is not an individual-centred explanation of religious commitment?

    a. reflection

    b. socialization

    c. deprivation

    d. salvation

13. The early social scientists were convinced that religion's days were numbered and that it would just be a matter of time before it was discarded in favour of science. Through the _____ the widespread consensus was that religion's influence was declining and that Canadians and people in other technologically advanced countries were leaving religion behind. Those observers proved to be wrong.

    a. 1950s

    b. 1960s

    c. 1970s

    d. 1980s

14. _____ dealt with such major themes as religious organization and the relationship between religion and social class. He reflected on religious leadership and the important process whereby a personal following is transformed into a permanent congregation, which he referred to as _____.

    a. Marx; opium of the masses

    b. Durkheim; the sacred and the profane

    c. Freud; the bonding stage

    d. Weber; routinization

15. In sociological terms, religious organizations are no different from other social organizations. Therefore, there has been a growing tendency to analyze religious groups by making use of the same frameworks we use in studying social organizations in general. With that in mind, which of the following is false?

    a. The Roman Catholic Church is a "multinational corporation."

    b. The United Church is a company that is Canadian-owned and -operated.

    c. The Methodist Church is a rural monopoly.

    d. The Baptist Union of Western Canada is a regional company.

Critical Thinking

1. As you've probably already gathered, much of the difficulty in conducting sociological research lies with the definition and measurement of the concept that you're trying to measure, and religion is no exception. If you were trying to determine levels of religiosity among Canadian adults, how would you define and measure religion? If your study happened to fall close to a religious holiday, such as Easter or Diwali, would your definition change? Why or why not?

2. Events such as the terrorist attacks on September 11, 2001, along with ongoing conflict in many places around the world, serve to remind us that religion is very much alive and viewed by some as a potential source of division and by others as something to which millions of people turn when they seek solace, meaning, and hope. How do your religious beliefs assist you with the struggles that go along with everyday life? If you're not a particularly religious person (depending on your definition), where do you find inspiration, hope, and comfort? Have your views on religion changed since the terrorist attacks?

3. In recent years, a number of Protestant "megachurches" have come into being in both Canada and the United States. They typically have seating for 1000–4000 people, are serviced by multiple full-time staffs, and have annual budgets in the millions of dollars. Does it bother you to study churches as groups or organizations or can you see the logic in treating churches in the same manner as any other organization? How does it make you feel to read about religion expressed in dollars and cents? Should we focus more on the spiritual and less on the monetary side of religion? For example, should the money that is being spent on creating new-age churches be spent on providing some basic necessities for those in need? Explain your answer.

4. I was surprised when I read some of the responses to the question as reported by Bibby, shown in Box 7.1 on page 160. The question posed was: "What will happen when I die?" Quite honestly, it's not something that I've given much thought to — have you? What do you think will happen to you when you die?

Web Links

The Prophet of Profit Sows the Seeds of Wealth
http://www.rickross.com/reference/general/general592.html
This site provides an excellent example of the relationship between religion and big business.

Method & Theory in the Study of Religion: Bibliography
http://eir.library.utoronto.ca/MandT/index.cfm
An extensive bibliographical index presented by the University of Toronto—an excellent resource for writing term papers on this topic.

Chapter 7

Religion
http://www.sfn.saskatoon.sk.ca/rel/0-religion.html
This is an excellent resource illuminating the evolution and diversity of religion.

Real International Statistics on Religion
http://religionstatistics.bravehost.com/statofrel1.htm
A global view of religion—highly informative.

Solutions

True or False?

1. F
2. T
3. T
4. F
5. T
6. F
7. T
8. T
9. T
10. F

Multiple Choice

1. B
2. D
3. A
4. A
5. B
6. D
7. C
8. B
9. D
10. C
11. B
12. D
13. B
14. D
15. C

Chapter 8

Social Stratification

Chapter Introduction

If you won $13 million in the lottery, how would it affect your social class? Though you'd likely move to a nicer house and drive a better car, do you think that your winnings would gain you entry into the world of the wealthy elite? Can you imagine getting an invitation to dine with Bill Gates or the Bronfmans? I can't imagine that you would. Sociologists study social class for a variety of reasons and they almost always come up with a variety of interesting results, but one thing is usually very certain — there is a distinct difference between classes in Canada and around the world and this difference is made up of more than just money. The movie *Trading Places* with Eddie Murphy and Dan Aykroyd is an exaggerated example of the stratification system that exists in most societies today and even though it's your basic Hollywood story, it does have an air of reality about it.

In this chapter, you'll learn about some of the ways in which sociologists study stratification and the theories that attempt to explain why inequalities exist in society. Additionally, you'll take a look at occupational and class structures, as well as material inequality in Canada. It really is amazing to see the disparities that exist between classes. Lastly, you'll investigate whether or not inequality has been increasing in the recent past.

Learning Objectives

At the conclusion of this chapter, you should be able to discuss or write about the following, without having to rely on the textbook:

1. Persistent patterns of social inequality within a society are referred to as a structure of social stratification. Some social hierarchies within a society are based on ascribed statuses such as gender, race, or age, which are typically assigned to an individual at birth. Other social hierarchies are based on achieved statuses, which mark how well an individual has performed within the same role.

2. A society in which considerable social mobility between statuses is possible is said to have an open system of stratification.

3. Karl Marx emphasized the exploitation of the working class by the owners of the means of production and the capacity of class conflict to generate social change. Max Weber also put considerable emphasis on the power that resides in ownership of property, but argued that other hierarchies, those of prestige and political power, are influential as well.

4. The structural–functionalist theory of social stratification suggests that inequality is both inevitable and functionally necessary for a society, ensuring that the most qualified individuals are selected to fill the most important and most rewarding roles. Power differences are downplayed in this theory, as is conflict between social classes.

5. Examination of occupational shifts in Canada over the course of the past century reveals some of the changing features of Canada's stratification system. Studies of occupational mobility reveal

that Canada is a relatively open society. Even so, there is considerable evidence that class-based advantages are passed from one generation to the next.

6. A detailed analysis of material inequality in Canada reveals that ownership of wealth and property is highly concentrated and that income inequality is relatively high. There is considerable evidence that the poor and others near the bottom of the social hierarchies in our society enjoy fewer life-chances than do the well off. Because of their more limited access to social and material resources, the poor have seldom become an active force for social change.

7. Some theories of social stratification developed in the middle of the twentieth century suggested that material inequality was declining as the North American economy expanded. As unemployment rates rise, as part-time and temporary work becomes more common, and as governments cut back on social-assistance programs, evidence accumulates that material inequality is also slowly increasing in Canada.

Quiz Questions

True or False?

1. An ascribed status is connected with race, gender, age, and other factors that are not chosen or earned and that cannot be changed (for the most part).
   True or False

2. Marx identified two major classes — the capitalist class or proletariat, which owned the means of production — and the bourgeoisie, which exchanged its labour for wages.
   True or False

3. Since competition for wealth and power is virtually non-existent in countries that espouse a more socialist form of government, social stratification, in any form, is more commonly associated with capitalist countries.
   True or False

4. The economic hierarchy is obviously not completely closed, but it is relatively stable and permanent, and is composed of individuals with similar amounts of control over material resources.
   True or False

5. Marx reasoned that the value of a product sold was directly proportional to the average amount of labour needed to produce it. Thus, for example, an elegant piece of furniture was more valuable than its component pieces mainly because of the labour invested in it by the worker(s).
   True or False

6. Since Marx lived to see the emergence of white-collar workers, the growth of large private- and public-sector bureaucracies, and the growing power of trade unions, he was able to write about these alternative sources of power in a stratified capitalist society.
   True or False

7. According to Davis and Moore (1945), social inequality is both inevitable and functionally necessary for society.
   True or False

8. According to Marx, conflict in modern society was diffused across many different sets of competing groups and was much less likely to lead to significant social unrest.
   True or False

9. According to the 1992 report of the Economic Council of Canada, poverty is not a static status. A sizeable number of Canadians move in and out of poverty each year.
   True or False

10. Researchers still have not determined whether more Canadians are voluntarily choosing self-employment or are being pushed into it as a result of higher levels of unemployment and growing corporate and public-sector "downsizing."
    True or False

Multiple Choice

1. In a _____ everyone would have an equal opportunity to compete for higher-status positions and, presumably, those most capable would be awarded the highest rank.
   a. socialist system
   b. meritocracy
   c. democracy
   d. capitalist system

2. _____ updated the original Marxist model so it could be applied to the twentieth century.
   a. Erik Olin Wright
   b. Lenski
   c. Davis and Moore
   d. Dahrendorf

3. _____ refers to a position of an individual or family within an economic hierarchy, along with others who have roughly the same amount of control over access to economic or material resources.
   a. Status
   b. Prestige
   c. Societal level
   d. Class

4. On average, women earn about _____ percent of what men earn.
   a. 50
   b. 60
   c. 70
   d. 80

5. According to the writings of Marx, which of the following economic forces did not contribute to the creation of a class-based society?
   a. emergence of large mechanized factory-based systems of production
   b. movement of women from the home to the workplace
   c. rapid growth of cities as rural peasants left the land
   d. extreme material inequality caused by huge profits for factory owners and merchants and the poverty of labourers

6. Weber shared with Marx a belief that economic inequalities were central to the social stratification system, and that the ownership of _____ was a primary determinant of power, or the ability to impose one's wishes on others, to get them to do what one wants them to do.
   a. property
   b. wealth
   c. workers
   d. power

7. The most prominent occupational shift over the course of the twentieth century is the decline in _____ occupations.
   a. agricultural
   b. mining
   c. self-employed
   d. factory

8. Whereas capitalists might be conscious of their group interests, wage-labourers needed to become aware of their common enemy. They needed to be transformed from a "class in itself" to a "class for itself." Thus, _____ was an important social-psychological component of Marx's theory of social inequality and social change.
   a. class consciousness
   b. false consciousness
   c. total awareness
   d. solidarity

9. _____ refers to the occupational mobility that occurs within a society when better-qualified individuals move upward to replace those who are less qualified and who must consequently move downward.
   a. Circulatory mobility
   b. Vertical mobility
   c. Horizontal mobility
   d. Intergenerational mobility

10. Which of the following is not a factor in determining socioeconomic status?
    a. income
    b. education
    c. occupation
    d. gender

11. In 1968, sociologist John Porter predicted that in the future, the demand for people to fill highly skilled positions would exceed the supply of well-educated workers. Porter's fear seems ironic today, when almost 1 in _____ employed Canadians state that they are overqualified for their job.

    a. 3
    b. 4
    c. 8
    d. 10

12. Antoniou and Rowley (1986) have demonstrated that more than _____ of the largest Canadian-owned corporations were controlled by a single owner (holding 20% or more of the shares).

    a. one-quarter
    b. one-third
    c. two-thirds
    d. one-half

13. Which of the following is not a characteristic of Weber's typology of inequality?

    a. employment
    b. class
    c. status
    d. party

14. Marx argued that the value of goods produced by wage-labourers far exceeded the amount needed to pay their wages and the cost of raw material, technology, and other components of the means of production. He referred to this excess as _____.

    a. competitive advantage
    b. surplus labour
    c. surplus exchange
    d. surplus value

15. Dramatic changes in the status of various groups have occurred in this country over time. Although the practice was not nearly as widespread in Canada as in the United States, slaves were bought and sold in Canada until the _____. By then, slavery had disappeared in Canada and we now have laws against discrimination on the basis of race.

    a. 1600s
    b. 1700s
    c. 1800s
    d. 1900s

Critical Thinking

1. Descriptions of social structure that ignore the stratification system are clearly inadequate. Imagine describing Canadian society to someone from another country without referring to some features of stratification. Is this possible? Write a letter to a friend from another country who is asking what your country is like.

2. A child from a wealthy family graduates from an excellent high school in an affluent neighbourhood, completes a degree or two in a prestigious and costly university, and then begins a career in a high status, well-paying profession. Is this an example of someone achieving a deserved high-status position, or did the advantages of birth play some part in this success story? What do you think? Although some students may have monetary advantages over others, do they have any kind of learning advantage over other students?

3. Although some differences in pay might be justified to reimburse those who spend more years in school preparing for an occupation, are the huge income inequalities that we see in our society necessary? Why do women often earn less than men, even if they are doing the same type of work? Are movie stars, professional athletes, and chief executive officers with million-dollar-plus annual incomes more important to society than nurses, day-care workers, prison guards, and most other low-paid workers? Can you justify the great differences in salaries? If so, what is your reasoning?

4. Most discussions of poverty in Canada rely on the low income cut-off line, estimated by Statistics Canada on the basis of data obtained from its annual survey of consumer finances. How valid a measure is this? Should the level of poverty be measured strictly in terms of income? Should quality of life be included in the measure? If so, how would you define it and include it?

Web Links

Canadian Council on Social Development
http://www.ccsd.ca/home.htm
The Canadian Council on Social Development (CCSD) is a non-governmental, not-for-profit organization, which was founded in 1920. Their mission is to develop and promote progressive social policies inspired by social justice, equality, and the empowerment of individuals and communities.

Misconceptions about "Basic Needs" Poverty Lines
http://oldfraser.lexi.net/publications/forum/1999/02/basic_needs.html
The Fraser Institute was founded in 1974 to redirect public attention to the role markets can play in providing for the economic and social well-being of Canadians.

Income and Social Status
http://www.hc-sc.gc.ca/dca-dea/publications/healthy_dev_partb_1_e.html
The Division Childhood and Adolescence is a focal point for policy development, research, and strategic analysis of trends regarding broad determinants of health regarding children and youth in Canada.

Multiple Sources of Power — Class, Status, and Party
http://uregina.ca/~gingrich/o2302.htm
This is a more general approach than that of Marx, since relationship to a market includes groups such as financiers, debtors, professional groups such as lawyers or doctors, and landowners.

Solutions

13. A
14. D
15. C

True or False?

1. T
2. F
3. F
4. T
5. T
6. F
7. T
8. F
9. T
10. T

Multiple Choice

1. B
2. A
3. D
4. C
5. B
6. A
7. A
8. A
9. A
10. D
11. B
12. C

Chapter 9

Gender Inequality: Economic and Political Aspects

Chapter Introduction

Do you think that the career to which you're aspiring will be affected at all by your gender? Are you aware of the inequalities that exist between men and women, especially when it comes to paid and unpaid work? When was the last time that you thanked your Mom (or in a few cases, your Dad) for doing your laundry or cleaning up the kitchen? I can remember the first time that I ever heard a male telephone operator. I was really taken off guard because it was just so unheard of. I had the same reaction when I first saw a man behind a check-out counter in the grocery store. It's not like men weren't qualified or entitled to do those jobs, it was just that they had traditionally been performed by women and I wasn't accustomed to seeing men in these roles. It's strange that I would have had that reaction because, a long time ago, I trained to become a machinist and, for a while, was one of the few female machinists in Ontario. I learned a long time ago that the world of work was much different for women than it was for men. Though it's hard to believe, gender inequality still exists in Canada and it's likely to persist well into the twenty-first century.

This chapter begins with a definition of gender inequality and then explores the major dimensions of it in Canadian society, with specific reference to the home, the labour force, and politics. You'll learn all about gender inequality as it exists in the economic and political aspects of society as well. Much of what you read will probably astound you, and I hope that you get a good handle on the inequalities that you may have to face one day. The chapter ends on a bright note, though, as Brym discusses the actions, policies, and legislation that could reduce gender inequality in the future.

Learning Objectives

At the conclusion of this chapter, you should be able to discuss or write about the following, without having to rely on the textbook:

1. Many sociologists view the segregation of women and men into the private and public spheres as a very important source of gender inequality. Exclusion from the economic and political arenas of Canadian life can mean disadvantages in access to income, economic well-being, prestige, and power. Restricted in the past to the domestic sphere, women have been economically disadvantaged and have had little or no opportunity to influence legislation directly. In addition, unpaid work in the home has been considered low in prestige, or at least lower in value than their spouses' paid work.

2. During the twentieth century, women have entered the labour force and the political arena in ever-increasing numbers. Today, more than half of all women are in the labour force. Between the 1970s and the early 1990s, the labour-force participation rate of women more than doubled, and the number of elected women MPs quadrupled.

3. Although they do paid work, many women are still responsible for most of the meal preparation, cleaning, and laundry needs of their families. Consequently, women are more likely than men to work a double or triple "shift" every day.

4. In the labour force, women and men are occupationally segregated with women concentrated in jobs that are stereotyped as "women's jobs." Women are more likely than men to be employed in jobs that are part-time or otherwise non-standard. They earn less than men, on average, and their skills tend not to be fully recognized or fairly evaluated.

5. Women represent more than half of Canada's adult population, but only 20 percent of federally elected legislators.

6. Future generations will have to combat not only gender-role stereotypes, but ideologies and structures that privilege men and handicap women as well. In recent years, employment-equity and equal-pay-for-work-of-equal-value policies have been developed to remedy some of the inequalities in the labour force. Analysts have also documented the various ways in which women's participation and influence in the political area can be enhanced.

Quiz Questions

True or False?

1. Women are usually employed in lower-skilled jobs. Since higher-skilled jobs usually differ from lower-skilled jobs in pay and security, employment in lower-skilled jobs implies economic and quality-of-work inequalities between men and women.
   True or False

2. Nepotism refers to the social evaluation or ranking, by general consensus, of occupational activities and positions in a hierarchical order that reflects the degree of respect, honour, or deference the person engaged in the activity or occupying the position is to be accorded.
   True or False

3. Although women have entered politics and the paid labour force in increasing numbers over the past century, they still tend to be chiefly responsible for meal preparation, cleaning, laundry, and child-care.
   True or False

4. When women face invisible barriers in penetrating the highest levels of organizations where power is concentrated and exercised, it is referred to as the glass ceiling effect.
   True or False

5. Oversimplified beliefs that men and women, by virtue of their physical sex, possess different personality traits and, as a result, may behave differently and experience the world in different ways are called gender labels.
   True or False

6. Thelma McMormack (1975) suggests that female−male differences in voting interests result because men and women operate in different social cultures (which have been moulded by gender differences in socialization) and have different opportunities to participate in politics.
   True or False

7. Today, two-earner husband—wife families report average family incomes of over $65 000, or approximately 1.4 times the incomes of families where only the husband has employment earnings.
   True or False

8. Few observers of Canadian political life doubt that politics is still very much a male domain, as exemplified by the success of Sheila Copps. Her success was partly attributed to the fact that she "knows how to fight like a man." The emphasis on male traits in the world of politics indicates that women in politics are sex-stereotyped.
   True or False

9. Political representation is merely one way in which gender inequality can be amended. A candidate's political platform refers to the statements made and the actions taken — or not taken — by governments with respect to a given problem or set of problems.
   True or False

10. Gender discrimination is essentially a display of power in which one person attempts to control, and often succeeds in controlling, another through sexual overtures.
    True or False

Multiple Choice

1. Chris Jackson, a Statistics Canada economist, estimates that unpaid work, if done at the market for wages, would have been worth about _____ in 1992, or about one-third of the gross national product (the total value of market-produced goods and services).

   a. $6 billion

   b. $58 billion

   c. $136 billion

   d. $235 billion

2. The growing labour-force participation of women has changed the composition of the Canadian labour force. At the beginning of the twentieth century, women represented _____ workers in the labour force.

   a. one in seven

   b. two in seven

   c. four in seven

   d. six in seven

3. The fact that gender is learned and that its content is continually renewed and altered through social interaction has three implications. Which of the following is not one of them?

   a. Gender identification can often be manipulated to match a person's sex (for example, transgendered individuals).

   b. Gender identities and behaviours are not stable and fixed.

   c. Gender identities and gender-specific behaviours are not always congruent with the sex assigned at birth.

   d. Gender identities and behaviours are not binary and polar opposites.

4. Which of the following did not influence changes in the labour-force participation rate of Canadian women?
   a. women choosing to marry at an older age
   b. increased demand for workers in service jobs
   c. decreases in the number of children born
   d. increased financial pressures on the family

5. Canada's fertility rates _____ during the 1930s and early 1940s as a result of the Depression and World War II.
   a. increased substantially
   b. decreased substantially
   c. stayed the same
   d. were not measured

6. Observers have offered four sets of explanations for the pay gap between women and men. Which of the following is not one of them?
   a. biological differences, leading to job discrimination
   b. gender differences in the type of work performed
   c. societal devaluation of women's work
   d. gender differences in the characteristics that influence pay rates

7. Data from the 1996 census show that women are still more likely than men to do unpaid work involving home maintenance and child care. For example, in 1996 _____ of all women were spending 30 hours or more on housework, compared to 7% of all men.
   a. 15%
   b. 25%
   c. 45%
   d. 55%

8. _____ refers to the process whereby employers make decisions about whether to hire and how much to pay any given woman on the basis of the employers' perceptions of the average characteristics of all women.
   a. Gender discrimination
   b. Statistical discrimination
   c. Nepotism
   d. Selective discrimination

9. Compared with men at every age, women in the labour force are much more likely to be part-time workers. During the past two decades, women have consistently made up _____ of the part-time labour force.
   a. 28%
   b. 46%
   c. 70%
   d. 81%

10. Which of the following is not a characteristic of media descriptions of female politicians?

    a. They use feminine traits to manipulate their public image.

    b. They fail to recognize the prior political activities of female politicians, with the result that the women's histories of acquiring competency remain unknown.

    c. They suggest that female politicians are responsible for women's issues, when, in fact, gender interests may or may not be on the agenda of any politician, male or female.

    d. They use the term feminism or feminist to denote negative personal characteristics.

11. State intervention influences the magnitude of gender inequality and sustains or minimizes male relations of power over women in three areas. Which of the following is not one of them?

    a. reproduction

    b. family

    c. professional sports

    d. the labour force

12. _____ refers to both the body of thought on the cause and nature of women's disadvantages and subordinate position in society and to efforts to minimize or eliminate that subordination.

    a. Affirmative action

    b. Radical inequality

    c. Feminism

    d. Employment equity

13. _____ is the result of the general belief that men are superior to women and may impose their will on women.

    a. Discrimination

    b. Sexual harassment

    c. Inequality

    d. Domination

14. Sociologists use the term _____ to refer to the behaviours that are expected of people occupying particular social positions. For example, in the 1950s, the attitudes and activities expected of women were those of wives and mothers.

    a. gender specificity

    b. discrimination

    c. gender roles

    d. gender status

15. Multiracial feminism contributes to our understanding of gender inequality in three ways. Which of the following is not one of them?

    a. It supports the ideological tenets of a matriarchal society.

    b. It highlights differences among women in terms of gender inequality.

    c. It points out that women of specific races and in certain class locations are in positions of power and domination over other groups of women.

    d. It emphasizes that solutions to gender inequality vary according to the location of groups of women in the matrix of domination.

Critical Thinking

1. High wages, low wages, huge differences in wages: What do you think wages will be like when you graduate? Will the difference in wages between men and women still be as great?

2. A committee headed by Ian Newbould, president of Mount Allison University, found that New Brunswick home-care workers are the lowest paid in the country, receiving between $5.50 and $7.50 an hour. Why would anyone work for such low wages? How can these wages be justified in an occupation that is so important?

3. According to liberal feminism, gender inequalities are caused and perpetuated by gender stereotyping and the division of work in to "women's jobs" and "men's jobs." For them, gender inequality can be achieved by (1) fighting and removing gender stereotyping and discrimination in education and at paid work and (2) by changing laws so that men and women have equal opportunities in the labour force and in politics. These solutions would definitely make an impact on gender inequality. Suppose for a day that you were a liberal feminist. How would you go about implementing these changes? What conditions must be present, in order for these changes to occur?

4. The discrepancy between men and women that exists in the realm of housework remains unchallenged. What would happen if housework became paid labour? In your opinion, would the percentage of men who spend time on housework increase? Why or why not?

5. Are you planning to enter a gender-specific occupation? Are you aware of any obstacles that you may have to face if you do so? Have you developed a strategy to conquer them?

Web Links

Pay Equity Review: Introduction
http://www.payequityreview.gc.ca/1200-e.html
This review of pay equity gives us a collective opportunity to assess, review, and discuss options with a broad range of individuals and organizations on how the current federal pay equity policy and legislative structure can be improved.

Pay Equity Commission: Interactives: Women and Work Quiz
http://www.gov.on.ca/lab/pec/peo/english/quiz/quiz16.html
Try this quiz to test your knowledge of women and work.

Women in Canada 2000
http://www.statcan.ca/english/ads/89-503-XPE/index.htm
As a quick reference, the millennial edition of Women in Canada uses relevant statistics and clear analysis from Statistics Canada to provide you with input and facts.

Rebel Dad: The Stay-At-Home Dad Revolution
http://www.rebeldad.com/2003_11_01_archive.html
Is the grass always greener? A refreshing twist on the traditional roles of husbands and wives.

Solutions

True or False?

1. T
2. F
3. T
4. T
5. F
6. F
7. T
8. T
9. F
10. F

Multiple Choice

1. D
2. A
3. A
4. A
5. B
6. A
7. B
8. B
9. C
10. A
11. C
12. C
13. B
14. C
15. A

Chapter 10

Race and Ethnic Relations

Chapter Introduction

Could you imagine having to eat the same food every day? What would our world be like if everyone had the same skin colour, taste in food, and chances for employability? I think that it would be a very boring world indeed. One of the best things about going to the Canadian National Exhibition is the food building and, as I get older, I find that I spend more time in there than I do in the line-up to get on a ride. Can you imagine how dull life would be if it weren't for the diversity that fuels our minds with wonder and feeds our soul with a plethora of music and colour? A trip to Toronto is always like a trip to another world for me. I could spend hours (and sometimes have) just walking up and down the busy streets, taking in the atmosphere and aroma of all the different cultures. I feel very proud to be living in a country that celebrates the differences among people. Although racism, discrimination, and prejudice still exist, I think that they diminish substantially with every generation and I hope that you will raise your children to appreciate the diversity that we have come to call home.

This chapter examines what sociologists mean by terms such as *ethnicity*, *race*, and *racism* and then discusses various theoretical approaches to the study of ethnic and racial relations. Additionally, the author investigates three main forms of ethnic relations in Canada in order to show how power and resource imbalances play an important part in structuring the relationships among groups.

Learning Objectives

At the conclusion of this chapter, you should be able to discuss or write about the following, without having to rely on the textbook:

1. Ethnic categories and identities are not fixed and unchanging; they evolve socially and historically.

2. Racism refers to certain kinds of ideas and to certain kinds of institutional practices. Institutional racism refers to circumstances where social institutions operate or once operated on the basis of racist ideas.

3. Racism, prejudice, and discrimination have been analyzed from different sociological perspectives. Social psychological theories, primordialism, normative theories, and power-conflict theories each offer different interpretations of ethnic and racial hostility.

4. The terms used to describe Aboriginal people are socially negotiated and change because of shifts in the power relations among groups.

5. The culture of poverty thesis was used in the 1970s as a way of explaining the poor socioeconomic conditions of Aboriginal people. Problems with the culture of poverty thesis led to the development of the internal colonial model, a variant of conflict theory. Conflict and feminist sociologists are beginning to be more interested in class and gender diversity within the Aboriginal population.

6. French–English relations in Canada are not about power relations.

7. There are debates in the nationalist movement about who is Quebecois. Tensions exist between ethnic and civic nationalists. Minorities in Quebec fear that they will not be included in the definition of a sovereign Quebec nation.

8. During the nineteenth century, immigrants contributed to capitalist state formation. Now, immigrants contribute to the social and economic reproduction of Canadian society.

9. There are six main variables that have shaped immigrant selection in Canada: social class, ethnic and racial stereotypes, geopolitical considerations, humanitarianism, pubic opinion and security considerations. Immigrants are categorized as refugees, family class, or independents. Independent immigrants are selected on the basis of a point system.

10. John Porter argued that Canada was a vertical mosaic, a social structure where ethnic groups occupy different and unequal positions within the stratification system. Evidence suggests that the vertical mosaic is declining in importance — at least for European immigrants and people born in Canada. Discrimination against visible-minority immigrants is still a problem.

Quiz Questions

True or False?

1. The sociology of ethnic and racial relations concerns primarily the study of how power and resources are unequally distributed among ethnic and racial groups.
    True or False

2. Traditionally, sociologists defined discrimination as "the belief that humans are subdivided into distinct hereditary groups that are innately different in their social behaviour and mental capacities and that can therefore be ranked as superior or inferior."
    True or False

3. Until 1985, Indian women who married non-Indian men, along with their children, lost their federally recognized Indian status; they became marginalized Indians.
    True or False

4. The internal colonial model is the most popular variant of the conflict approach. It analyzes the problem of inequality in terms of power imbalances and the exploitation of Aboriginal people and lands by white society.
    True or False

5. Barker (1981) argued that the new ethnicity involves the beliefs that although some groups of people cannot be ranked biologically, with some being inferior and some superior, they are naturally different from each other, and that social problems are created when different groups try to live together.
    True or False

6. According to Marxists, racism is ideological insofar as it is used by capitalists to mystify social reality and justify the exploitation and the unequal treatment of groups of people.
    True or False

7. The concept of a culture of poverty was first developed by Oscar Lewis (1961), an American anthropologist interested in explaining the slow pace at which Mexican-Americans and Puerto Ricans were being assimilated into U.S. society.
    True or False

8. Menno Boldt (1993) argues that most Indian reserves are comprised of a three-class social order: a very small elite class, a slightly larger middle class consisting of those who possess a skill or trade, and a large lower class comprising destitute, dependent, and powerless people.
    True or False

9. Aboriginal people in Canada are made up of Indians, Metis, and Inuit.
    True or False

10. Though written in 1965, John Porter's description of Canada as a vertical mosaic is still very indicative of the way in which ethnic groups tend to occupy different and unequal positions in the stratification system.
    True or False

Multiple Choice

1. A survey conducted in 1990 by Decima Research Ltd. showed that _____ percent of Canadians agreed with the statement "All races are created equal."

    a. 60

    b. 70

    c. 80

    d. 90

2. The _____ thesis suggests that ethnic and racial attachments reflect an innate tendency for people to seek out, and associate with, others who are similar in language, culture, beliefs, ancestry, and appearance.

    a. frustration-aggression

    b. essentialist

    c. sociobiologist

    d. primordialist

3. Statistical evidence shows that Aboriginal peoples are the most socially and economically disadvantaged groups in the country. About _____ of all existing housing for status Indians who live on reserves fails to meet the basic standards for safe and healthy living, such as running water, central heating, sewer connections or septic tanks, and electricity.

    a. one-quarter

    b. one-third

    c. one-half

    d. three-quarters

4. Since the 1950s, the scientific consensus is that _____.
   a. racial prejudice is socially acquired
   b. racial classifications of humanity are arbitrary
   c. genetic differences between groups are small
   d. genetic differences are behaviourally insignificant

5. _____ theories of ethnic and racial prejudices concentrate on the way in which prejudices are transmitted through socialization and the social circumstances that compel discriminatory behaviour.
   a. Normative
   b. Primordialism
   c. Power conflict
   d. Social psychology

6. Which of the following is not true of the split labour-market theory?
   a. It argues that Orthodox Marxism tends to assume that the capitalist class is all-powerful and that other classes play no role in the development of racist thinking.
   b. Orthodox Marxism portrays racism in overly conspiratorial terms.
   c. Orthodox Marxism has trouble explaining why racialized conflict so often results in exclusionary practices — practices that deny employers access to cheaper, more exploitable labour.
   d. Orthodox Marxism, because of its reliance on economics, fails to explain the social realities that surround racism.

7. Skilled immigrant workers are selected by the federal government on the basis of their ability to meet certain minimum work experience requirements, to prove that they have enough funds to support themselves and their family members in Canada, and merit is measured by the points system. An applicant has to earn a minimum of _____ out of 100 points to "pass" and potentially gain admission to Canada as a skilled worker.
   a. 55
   b. 65
   c. 75
   d. 85

8. There are three main empirical findings that are relevant to the debate about the vertical mosaic in present-day Canada. Which of the following is not one of them?
   a. Canadian society is much more open that it once was in terms of the social evaluation of European immigrants and their descendents.
   b. Mandatory retirement at age 65 has diminished the potential earning years of those immigrants who would like to continue working.
   c. The earnings and occupational distributions of visible-minority men and women who are born in Canada are comparable to those of the charter groups and of other Europeans.
   d. The pattern of gender visible-minority differences in earnings is even more evident where immigrants are concerned.

9. _____ are made up of people who identify themselves, or who are identified by others, as belonging to the same ancestral or cultural group.

    a. Marginal groups

    b. Races

    c. Ethnic groups

    d. Subcultures

10. The concept of institutional racism refers to "discriminatory racial practice built into such prominent structures as the political, economic, and education systems." Which of the following is not a form of institutional racism?

    a. circumstances where institutional practices are based on explicitly racist ideas

    b. circumstances where societal institutions such as religion and education fail to promote racial integration

    c. circumstances where institutional practices arose from but are no longer sustained by racist ideas

    d. circumstances where institutions unintentionally restrict the life-chances of certain groups through a variety of seemingly neutral rules, regulations, and procedures

11. Split labour market theory was developed by Edna Bonacich because of the limitations of orthodox Marxism in analyzing racism. Which of the following is not one of her criticisms?

    a. Marxism tends to assume that the capitalist class is all-powerful, and that other classes play no role in the development of racist thinking.

    b. Because Marx's theories are largely based on economics, they can't be used as a viable tool in explaining racism.

    c. Marxism portrays racism in overly conspiratorial terms.

    d. Marxism has trouble explaining why racialized conflict so often results in exclusionary practices.

12. Which of the following is not a characteristic displayed in Indian culture, according to Oscar Lewis's framework?

    a. a present rather than a future time-orientation

    b. an over-emphasis on folklore and legend

    c. a high value on mutual aid without the expectation of return

    d. a lack of emphasis on the possession of material goods

13. _____ argue that racism is an ideology — a set of statements shaped by one's economic interests about the way the social world "really works."

    a. Structural functionalists

    b. Politicians

    c. Orthodox Marxists

    d. Normative theorists

14. Sociologists recognize that while we cannot change our birth parents, and generally cannot change our skin colour, we do not necessarily have fixed and unalterable ethnic and racial characteristics or identities. They believe that it is more useful to see race and ethnicity as certain kinds of _____ status.

    a. ascribed

    b. achieved

    c. elite

    d. conflicting

15. There are three main categories of immigrants in Canada. Which of the following is not one of them?

    a. refugees

    b. family class

    c. adoptive

    d. independent

Critical Thinking

1. The issue of multiculturalism is one that often sparks heated discussions. In many cases, marriage within your race is the only acceptable form of marriage. Some Canadians believe that race relations in Canada are getting worse, and on the other end of the spectrum, many describe the joys of living in a multi-ethnic country. Often I find that students are hesitant to admit their true feelings about Canada's immigration policies because they fear being labelled as racist or prejudiced. This learning guide is a very safe place to investigate how you really feel about this issue. Be honest with yourself and describe how you feel about multiculturalism in Canada. Have your feelings changed since you've started post-secondary education?

2. In this time of political correctness, it often seems as though I'm walking on eggshells, when I attend a multicultural function. I always worry that I'm going to say the wrong thing, and embarrass myself or others. It's probably because I grew up and still live in a relatively small city and I'm not used to the cultural diversity that exists in Toronto or other large cities, but I sometimes have "Archie Bunker" nightmares where I innocently slip and offend someone. Do you ever feel the same way? How do you make sure that you maintain political correctness?

3. Since 1962, ethnic and racial stereotyping in selecting new immigrants has become less important. Canadian immigration policy is now more open in terms of ethnic and racial origins of immigrants. Before 1961, Europeans made up over 90% of total immigrants to Canada. In 2001, immigrants from Europe made up 17.26% of the total flow of immigrants to Canada. Examine Table 10.3 on page 262 to take a closer look at the incredible changes that have occurred over time. How can you account for these changes? Do you think that Canada's stand on multiculturalism has affected both the number of immigrants entering Canada and also the countries from which they come?

4. The term "Quiet Revolution" describes the social, political, and cultural changes that occurred in Quebec in the 1960s, in part because of the initiatives of a new middle class. It's hard to believe, four decades later, that the politics of this situation are still unresolved. In your opinion, can the issue of Quebec's separation be resolved? What are the sociological implications of separation?

Web Links

The About Canada Publication
http://www.mta.ca/faculty/arts/canadian_studies/english/archived/
theaboutcanadapublication.html
The ABOUT CANADA publication is a series of brief analytical overviews of modern Canadian issues and culture.

Citizenship and Immigration Canada
http://www.cic.gc.ca/
Canada's citizenship and immigration programs help build a community of citizens respected throughout the world.

Research Areas — Ethnicity & Racism
http://www.icescolombo.org/research1.htm
Since its establishment in 1982, the International Centre for Ethnic Studies, (ICES), Colombo has striven to evolve a model of historically sensitive, theoretical, and empirical research on ethnicity, and related socioeconomic, political, and cultural process

Culture and Ethnicity in Philosophy
http://pegasus.cc.ucf.edu/~janzb/philcult/
This site gathers resources relevant to the philosophical study of culture and ethnicity. Included here are links to philosophy in specific cultures, philosophical anthropology, and cross-cultural and intercultural philosophy.

Solutions

True or False?

1. T
2. F
3. F
4. T
5. F
6. T
7. T
8. F
9. T
10. F

Multiple Choice

1. D
2. D
3. D
4. A
5. A
6. D
7. C
8. B
9. C
10. B
11. B
12. B
13. C
14. B
15. C

Chapter 11

Inequality among Nations: Perspectives on Development

Chapter Introduction

How often do you think of what's going on around the world? Are the commercials asking you to sponsor a child in a Third World country the only reminders that extreme poverty is prevalent in a large part of the world? In 2003, Stephen Lewis was named by *Maclean's* magazine as Man of the Year in Canada. It is the first year that this timely publication has ever held this competition. Lewis has been on the Canadian scene for years and, in this issue, is recognized for his many accomplishments. His fight to win the battle against HIV/AIDS in Africa figures prominently in his profile. In a continent that is ravaged by disease and unsettlement, Lewis finds a delicate thread of hope to which everyone clings, often in the smile of a child or in the eyes of a grandmother who has lost her children to this dreadful disease. Desperate for donations, he says "If our governments were one-tenth as generous as average Canadians, the problem would be solved. Truthfully, when I see what we can accomplish with money on the ground, it's the only time in my life that I have wished I was Bill Gates." (*Maclean's*, 2003).

This chapter allows you to look at those countries from a developmental perspective and gives you an understanding of why the poverty remains. By exploring the competing perspectives on why there are rich and poor countries, we gain a greater understanding of what can be done to enable everyone to fully develop their own unique capacities. Much of this discussion seems to be based in economics, and sociological founders such as Karl Marx and Max Weber show that social, political, and cultural issues must be understood in relation to economics. This chapter looks at the four major perspectives against the historical record and offers a more balanced approach to understanding global inequality.

Learning Objectives

1. The search by transnational corporations for profits leads to shifts between rich and poor countries and the location of work, and has massive implications for citizens' well-being.

2. Ways of measuring material and nonmaterial well-being show great disparities between rich and poor countries, as well as between classes and genders within countries.

3. In 1750, there were no substantial gaps in living standards and levels of productivity among countries. Today's poor countries are primarily those once colonized by the West.

4. The assumptions of liberalism and modernization theory about free markets and capitalist development are adopted by the International Monetary Fund (IMF), transnational corporations, and the U.S. government, but do not live up to their promises for improving the well-being of most citizens of the Third World.

5. Dependency theory emphasizes the economic and political obstacles to development in the Third World that derive from foreign control.

6. Domestic control of corporations and activist governments were the keys to success in the spectacular development breakthroughs that mark the histories of South Korea and Sweden.

7. More democratic, egalitarian, and supportive policies for development will benefit all countries. Kerala is a good example of this. Those in the rich North may have to sacrifice some material wealth to share more around the world and ensure ecological sustainability.

Quiz Questions

True or False?

1. The Washington consensus is a version of Western-centric approaches and is dominant in Canada and other advanced capitalist countries. The belief of this approach is that most countries in the world are poor because Western capitalist institutions and values have not penetrated them deeply enough.
   True or False

2. Transnational corporations are prepared to shift the site of work in order to maximize profits. This has massive favourable opportunities for peoples' employment and well-being.
   True or False

3. Handicrafts still accounted for half of world industrial output in 1900. Capitalist industrialization occurred with such a rapid pace and in such concentrated areas that it created dominant economic powers that subjugated and destroyed existing industry in regions that would eventually become the Third World.
   True or False

4. Liberalism is blind to power inequalities and how they affect equality or opportunity. Its principles are drawn from idealized models of perfect markets. By embracing the world of economic models and ignoring the real world of vastly unequal power, liberalism justifies the privileges of the already powerful.
   True or False

5. Economists usually measure growth and living standards using the GNP or the GDP. For the most part, these terms are interchangeable. GDP is the value of all goods and services produced in a country in a year, according to official statistics of market income.
   True or False

6. Globalization comprises the processes leading towards greater world integration economically, politically, socially, culturally, in government policies, in communications, and in consciousness. It is a contested term that almost always means a weakening of nations and states.
   True or False

7. Disparities between rich and poor countries are enormous. Life expectancy is 60 years in the Third World, compared to 78 years in advanced capitalist countries.
   True or False

8. The weakness of Gerschenkron's (1962) perspective is that it places too much emphasis on the power and the motivation of the advanced states and leading transnationals to maintain the advantages that they already possess.
    True or False

9. A child born in the United States or Canada will consume, on average, 10 times the resources and produce 10 times the pollution of a child born in Bangladesh or Bolivia.
    True or False

10. Capitalism contains the seeds of its own destruction, wrote Marx. As capitalism replaces less efficient modes of production, such as feudalism, and displaces classes, such as serfs, it creates, in ever-larger numbers, communities of wage earners who have to sell their labour power as a commodity to enrich capitalists.
    True or False

Multiple Choice

1. In 1750, most children born in London did not live to see their _____ birthday.
    a. fourth
    b. fifth
    c. sixth
    d. seventh

2. The Industrial Revolution had its roots in the _____ industry. It was a peculiar industry to transform the world.
    a. forest
    b. mining
    c. agricultural
    d. cotton

3. The_____ was set up in 1944 to facilitate international trade and corporate investment by making national currencies readily convertible into the currencies of other member countries.
    a. IMF
    b. World Bank
    c. EU
    d. OECD

4. Under _____, states are oriented more to the rights of transnational corporations than to the demands of voters, and are locked up in neo-liberal principles by structural adjustment programs in the "South" and international institutions in the "North."
    a. capitalism
    b. socialism
    c. globlalism
    d. democracy

5. In the eighteenth and nineteenth centuries, _____ was the most remote of the three fabled "rich" countries of Asia that were coveted by the West.

    a. Japan

    b. Hong Kong

    c. Singapore

    d. Taiwan

6. In Mexico, liberal policies replaced nationalist economic policies and income gaps grew. From 1984 to 1995, the richest _____ of Mexicans increased their share of national income from 33% to 43%, whereas the share of the bottom 40% fell from 14% to 7%.

    a. 5%

    b. 10%

    c. 15%

    d. 18%

7. Health care is of extreme importance when considering the fate of a nation. What will motivate health improvements if the keys are dietary and lifestyle changes, environmental protection, and an end to poverty and illiteracy from which corporations do not profit? More than _____ children die annually of easily preventable diseases because no one pays for their immunizations during the first year of life.

    a. 500 000

    b. 1 000 000

    c. 1 500 000

    d. 2 000 000

8. In attempting to explain global inequalities, sociologists look largely to four main perspectives. Both the "Western-centric" and "anti-imperialist" contain valuable insights but both ignore important factors. The Washington consensus is a version of Western-centric approaches and is dominant in _____ and other advanced capitalist countries.

    a. Canada

    b. the United States

    c. Germany

    d. France

9. All is not always what it appears to be. If national incomes rise, do middle- and low-income people benefit? Not necessarily. National averages hide poverty by lumping together the incomes of the rich and the poor. For example, Bill Gates's assets are roughly _____. The Human Development Reports weigh the life-sustaining needs of the poorest billions against the economic freedoms of the richest few.

    a. US$4 billion

    b. US$28 billion

    c. US$52 billion

    d. US$63 billion

10. The concept of globalization hides the major actors of the past two centuries: corporations pursuing profits and the most powerful states. Since 1945, supranational institutions that support corporate rights emerged as a third set of actors shaping world development. Which of the following is not one of them?

    a. WTO

    b. IMF

    c. EU

    d. G-7 countries

11. The structural differences between core and periphery, the UN Economic Commission for Latin America argued, led to_____, in which the "terms of trade" between the periphery's resources and the core's finished goods worsen. This means that, over time, peripheral countries must export more and more resources in order to import a given number of finished products.

    a. increased debt

    b. greater dependence

    c. unequal exchange

    d. increased exports

12. Since 1960, _____ went from an impoverished, war-torn country with a few natural resources to a sophisticated exporter of automobiles and electronics. Living standards are getting close to Canadian levels.

    a. China

    b. Japan

    c. South Korea

    d. Sweden

13. _____ has one of the greatest gaps between rich and poor. The richest 1% control 50% of the nation's income, while the poorest half live on just 10% of the country's income.

    a. Brazil

    b. Africa

    c. Korea

    d. Argentina

14. Gender profoundly affects one's life-chances. The health risks of pregnancy are the greatest for poor women. Poor women face a risk of dying during pregnancy and birth that is up to _____ times higher than for women in developed nations.

    a. 200

    b. 400

    c. 600

    d. 800

15. Liberalism is the classical doctrine that equates capitalism with freedom and distrusts the power of governments. This perspective is based on six assumptions that are all contested by other perspectives. Which of the following is not one of them?

    a. Free markets for capital, labour, and resources separate productive from unproductive firms more efficiently than government.

    b. For the global market to work efficiently there should be no place for the nation or any collectivity larger than the firm.

    c. Profits are the best incentive for innovation and business efficiency, but in order to maximize them and distribute them appropriately, there should be limits to capital accumulation and the extent to which a single individual or corporation controls a country's economy.

    d. Market freedom leads to the greatest human freedom, which is threatened by government power.

Critical Thinking

1. The National Security Strategy declared that the United States has the right to make "pre-emptive strikes" not only against countries that pose an immediate risk, but also against any country that poses a potential risk. Amongst the United States' "non-negotiable demands" is that all other countries must have "respect for private property" — in other words, for U.S. transnational corporations abroad. In your opinion, does this doctrine of pre-emptive war take away the diplomacy, the self-determination, and the sovereignty rights of other countries? It seems as though other nations are more oriented to the rights of transnational corporations than to the demands of their voters. What does this say about ethnocentrism?

2. Proponents of the Western-centric approaches believe that most countries in the world are poor because Western capitalist institutions and values have not penetrated them deeply enough. Supporters of the anti-imperialist perspectives feel that most countries are poor because Western capitalism and imperialism have penetrated them too deeply. Which perspective, if either, do you support? What are your reasons?

3. World markets do not work according to textbook formulas. Real markets are dominated by a few giant companies that use monopoly positions to capture excess profits. Controlled by dominant capitalist countries, the IMF and the World Bank determine the policies of Third World governments. Instead of allowing governments to develop their own repayment policies, the IMF imposes rigid prescriptions that benefit Northern bankers and local, often corrupt, elites. Why is what appears to be extortion tolerated in our society today?

4. In 1999 the World Bank fired Joseph Stiglitz, the Bank's chief economist because he expressed doubts about World Bank and IMF neo-liberal policies. The World Bank and the IMF, though separate institutions, are linked by "triggers." For example, taking a World Bank loan to build a school "triggers" a requirement to accept every conditionality — on average, 111 per nation — laid down by both the World Bank and IMF. Loans and assistance packages to countries in

81

economic trouble are, says the World Bank, designed after careful in-country investigation. Joseph Stiglitz disagrees and told an investigative journalist that the "investigation" consists of close inspection of a country's five-star hotels. Though he did lose his job, in 2001 he won the Nobel Peace Prize for Economics. If you were Joseph Stiglitz, would you have made the same decision that he did? What are the implications of his actions?

Web Links

Online NewsHour: Striking First — July 1, 2002
http://www.pbs.org/newshour/bb/military/jan-june02/strikingfirst_7-01.html
PBS, headquartered in Alexandria, Virginia, is a private, non-profit media enterprise owned and operated by the U.S.'s 349 public television stations.

Joseph Stiglitz — Homepage
http://www-1.gsb.columbia.edu/faculty/jstiglitz/index.cfm
Joseph E. Stiglitz resigned from the World Bank in a cloud of controversy. He later went on to win the Nobel Peace Prize for Economics. You can learn more about it here.

IMF — International Monetary Fund Home Page
http://www.imf.org/
The IMF is an international organization of 184 member countries. It was established to promote international monetary cooperation, exchange stability, and orderly exchange arrangements. Check out this website to see how equally distributed the money is.

The World Bank Group
http://www.worldbank.org/
This website offers an abundance of information about global equality and inquality from the viewpoint of one of the world's largest moneylenders. How objective do you think this information is?

Solutions

True or False?

1. T
2. F
3. F
4. T
5. T
6. T
7. F
8. F
9. T
10. T

Multiple Choice

1. B
2. D
3. A
4. C
5. A
6. B
7. D
8. A
9. C
10. A
11. C
12. C
13. A
14. C
15. C

Chapter 12

Families

Chapter Introduction

Whenever I begin teaching, I introduce myself to my students and almost always tell them how lucky I am to have such a wonderful and supportive family. This doesn't usually get a reaction until I tell them that I'm the second youngest child of thirteen children! Big families are not very common these days and I guess you can say that like many familial arrangements in society today, my family doesn't fit into the neat little definition of the nuclear family that has been around for decades. I can't imagine a life without brothers or sisters. I have six sisters and originally I had six brothers, but two have joined my Dad in Heaven, so there are eleven of us left. Let me tell you that Christmas is a wild scene! Even though I have a very large family, I bet that the chances of your family being on television are no greater than mine. There's been a variety of television families and it seems as though we've traded in the Cleavers for the Osbournes. In my view, neither resembles my family and I suspect that they don't resemble yours either. Without doubt, the definition of the nuclear family is changing, and I think that it's about time.

In this chapter, the author reviews the dilemmas that many families face in light of the popular myths that surround them. Because family life is so familiar to us, we often accept the theories that explain it and the commonsense understandings of it without a second thought. Most families experience a variety of problems that are often swept under the rug and explained away by the personal, private characteristics of "human nature." In this chapter, you'll read about two patterns of family life that are very different from our own. In foraging societies, families lived in a communal setting and were based on reciprocity, where everyone shared the family chores. The social relations of the agricultural families were also the relations of production, where the chief economic relationship was that between the husband and wife. By the end of the chapter, you'll have learned how families have changed over time and evolved into the different family forms that we have in today's society.

Learning Objectives

At the conclusion of this chapter, you should be able to discuss or write about the following, without having to rely on the textbook:

1. Commonsense arguments hold that current dilemmas in family life, such as how women can balance the responsibilities of family and paid work and how men can succeed at breadwinning and do their share of the housework, are private individual problems. Similarly, family-values advocates argue that change by individuals is the solution to family problems. In the absence of a sociological analysis, the public sources of these problems — and of their potential solutions — remain unclear and unrecognized.

2. Although the nuclear family is common, it is not always responsible for child-care; often, the family is embedded in a larger household or community that collectively assumes responsibility for all the children of the group.

3. Family organization can be seen as loosely related to the organization of production, especially if family is defined as the sets of relationships that people create to meet the daily needs of adults and children.

4. In foraging societies, the nuclear family is embedded in a larger group that cooperates with respect to subsistence, consumption, and child-care. Paradoxically, the communal nature of these societies grants considerable autonomy to the individuals living in them.

5. In the agricultural societies of pre-industrial Europe, households were primarily units of production in which the need to survive took precedence over all else. Household composition, and even the texture of emotional life, reflected economic pressures.

6. Contemporary family patterns are the product of a particular history. Our history is marked by the development of an economy outside the household, in which the relations of paid employment are separated from the relations that provide for daily personal needs and the needs of children. A gendered division of labour corresponds to this separation.

7. As women have increasingly come to share the burden of family financial support, men have not proportionally increased the work that they do in the home. The fact that most jobs are geared to people who lack family responsibilities is partly what prevents men from taking on more housework — their time is too limited. However, ideas about gender also make men reluctant to do "women's work."

8. The gendered division of labour that makes it possible for nuclear families to care for young children involves significant liabilities for women, and even for children. The social isolation that full-time mothers experience, combined with the stress attached to their high-demand, low-control situation, reduces the quality of child-care that they are able to provide. Now that so many mothers are working outside the home, however, the problems associated with privatized responsibility for child-care may prove too burdensome, and government supports are likely to provide the only viable solution.

9. Because of fairly high rates of divorce and an increasing incidence of births to unmarried women, many Canadian children will spend some part of their lives in lone-parent families. Most problematic about this type of family is its typically low income and the resulting stress on the parent.

10. The policies of the Canadian state pertaining to families are premised on the assumption that the welfare of family members — even children — is not the responsibility of the government or of the community. Accordingly, family law in Canada now views marriage as the union of two individuals who are responsible for their own support, even in the case of a divorcing woman who was a full-time homemaker.

Quiz Questions

True or False?

1. Although conventional patterns are in decline, our society still seems to be organized around traditional nuclear families and 1950s gender roles. This is due in part because in the 1950s people married earlier, had more children, and were less likely to divorce than the generations that preceded and followed them.
    True or False

2. Commonsense solutions prescribe individual change and ignore the social context. In contrast, sociology uncovers the social origins of family patterns and the problems that they entail.
    True or False

3. Because of the biology of reproduction — which we take as "given" — is interpreted in different ways across different cultures, the role of the father in conception is recognized in virtually every culture.
    True or False

4. When "mothers' allowances" were started early in the twentieth century in Canada, they were paid only to widows — women clearly without men — even though other types of lone mothers were equally in need of assistance. Newer forms of social assistance have involved "man-in-the-house" rules, which disqualify any woman who appears to have man in her life.
    True or False

5. A key problem with the social conflict perspective as it relates to family life is its focus on how institutions create social order, and its consequent failure to analyze the tensions that can occur in family life that can generate social change.
    True or False

6. Evidence on family patterns across various cultures indicates that, although the nuclear family is common in many cultures, it is not always the unit that provides care for children. In many cultures, the nuclear family exists primarily to provide sex and companionship for adults.
    True or False

7. Comparisons of men's and women's physical and mental health in the 1960s and the 1970s show that women benefited from the care they received in marriage, while the work of personal care took a toll on men. Married women were significantly better off physically and mentally than single women, whereas the opposite was true for men.
    True or False

8. Generally, the conventional division of labour by sex has solved the problems created by an economy in which employers bear no direct responsibility for the welfare of their employees' families.
    True or False

9. People divorce largely because at least one spouse feels that something central to the marriage no longer exists — something such as sharing of responsibility or mutual caring. Men are more likely than women to initiate separation and divorce.
    True or False

10. Our family patterns developed out of the patterns that were typical of pre-capitalist agricultural societies so that the social relations of family life in pre-capitalist households — that is, relations between spouses, between parents and children, and among residents of the same household — were also the relations of production.
    True or False

Multiple Choice

1. Only in the _____ century did people begin to assume that romantic love, sex for the sake of pleasure, and marriage should be intimately bound together.
    a. 17th
    b. 18th
    c. 19th
    d. 20th

2. Because only about _____ of Canadian families in 1991 consisted of a married couple in which the man was the exclusive breadwinner, the woman was a full-time mother, and there were unmarried children living at home, concern about families has escalated.
    a. 5%
    b. 10%
    c. 15%
    d. 20%

3. _____ refers to feeding, clothing, and otherwise looking after people's subsistence needs, as well as nurturing and socializing children and emotionally supporting adults.
    a. Familial responsibility
    b. Cultural reproduction
    c. The hierarchy of needs
    d. Social reproduction

4. Today, women may have assumed part of the responsibility of breadwinning — in 1991 they contributed about _____ percent of family income — but they remained largely responsible for the housework.
    a. 5
    b. 17
    c. 26
    d. 35

5. The _____ was an unusually "familistic" decade: people married earlier, had more children, and were less likely to divorce than the generations that preceded and followed them.
    a. 1940s
    b. 1950s
    c. 1960s
    d. 1970s

6. Gaskell's (1983) findings indicate that girls prioritize domestic responsibilities largely because of the lack of _____ facing them.

    a. daycare

    b. education

    c. opportunity

    d. training

7. In practice, _____ call for policies that punish deviations from the nuclear-family ideal. They want to outlaw abortion, prohibit gay and lesbian marriages and parenthood, and encourage women to stay home with their children rather than provide funding for daycare facilities.

    a. moral majority voters

    b. anti-gay rights activists

    c. Roman Catholics

    d. family-values advocates

8. In view of the fact that women have entered the labour market in increasing numbers — and thus gained the possibility of self-support — and have been exposed to the climate of change brought about by the women's liberation movement, it is not surprising that divorce rates have risen. It is estimated that about _____ of marriages in Canada will end in divorce, which is considerably below rates in the United States and Sweden, but high when the consequences for children are considered.

    a. 10%

    b. 20%

    c. 30%

    d. 40%

9. _____ hold that, as with physical traits, social behaviour is inherited biologically — in other words, that behaviour can be linked to specific genetic configurations. Typically, they construct a story about the history of human evolution that assumes genetic encoding of behaviour — a problematic assumption since there is no evidence to support it.

    a. Evolutionists

    b. Sociobiologists

    c. Determinists

    d. Radical theorists

10. Although structural functionalism dominated the study of families until recently, there are obvious problems with this perspective. Which of the following is not one of them?

    a. Just because an institution performs a social function, there is no reason to assume that some other institution might not perform that function equally well.

    b. Its focus on how institutions create social order and its consequent failure to analyze the tensions in family life can generate social change.

    c. The functions that are emphasized allegedly meet the needs of society, but not necessarily, the individuals in it.

    d. It is predicated on the historical definition of the nuclear family, which is, for the most part, outdated and not indicative of current trends in Canadian society.

11. Whereas the absence of privatized family life empowered individuals in foraging societies, private ownership of the means of production and a considerable struggle to survive meant that agricultural societies had certain characteristics. Which is not one of them?

    a. All individuals were subordinated to the household enterprise.

    b. Elders held power and made most decisions for the clan.

    c. Women were subordinated to men.

    d. Children were subordinated to parents.

12. It is only in recent Western history that the family characteristics we take for granted coalesced — namely, the gendered division of labour. Which of the following does not described this division?

    a. Women provide care for children and members of the extended family.

    b. Women are primarily responsible for child-care and housework and men for financial provision.

    c. Motherhood is seen as women's primary vocation.

    d. Women provide emotional intensity as the foundation of family relations.

13. The trade-union movement responded to the straits of working-class life with a campaign for a _____, that is, a wage paid to a man sufficient to support a wife and children.

    a. decent wage

    b. family wage

    c. minimum wage

    d. wage based on commission

14. The majority of Canadian women are faced with the need to juggle the fundamentally incompatible demand of employment and family every day. The stress of their _____ of work generates considerable tension between women and their male partners.

    a. conflicting roles

    b. stereotyped duties

    c. expected load

    d. double day

15. Same-sex couples display characteristics that approximate family ideals. Their relationships are _____ likely to break up than heterosexual marriages and are no more likely to do so than cohabiting heterosexual couples.

    a. more
    b. less
    c. equally
    d. much more

Critical Thinking

1. "Although individuals make choices about whether to marry, have children, and so on, the social forces guiding them toward those decisions are so powerful that most individuals end up making the same choices." Do you agree or disagree with this statement? What if you're a woman who chooses voluntary childlessness, or a closeted gay in a heterosexual relationship? Do the pressures to conform that are pervasive throughout society wreak havoc on your own personal beliefs and desires? What does this statement say about individuality?

2. Research on various aspects of personal development shows that there are no significant differences between children of gay and lesbian parents and children of heterosexual parents. Do you find this result surprising? Why or why not? Do you think that children who have same-sex parents will face more adversity in life than children with heterosexual parents?

3. There is a growing conviction that being a full-time mother is bad for women and, consequently, for their children, and that men's physical absence from the home can also be detrimental to the social development of children, if their absence leads to emotional distance from the children. In the past, women who worked outside the home and left their children to daycare providers were chastised. Can valid arguments be made for both sides and, if so, what are they? With the increasing need for both parents to work outside of the home in order to live a comfortable life, is there a reasonable solution to this situation? If so, what is it?

4. What's your take on the Osbournes? I've heard both sides of the story from many of my students. Although they're crude and somewhat rough around the edges of conformity, they really do seem to love each other. Is this love enough to keep them in a stable familial relationship? Are they examples of positive role models?

Web Links

Crazy for Dysfunction
http://archive.salon.com/mwt/feature/2002/05/03/dysfunction/
Somewhere along the line, we traded the Cleavers for the Osbournes. Family angst and social stigma are new tickets to fame and fortune.

Children Come First: A Report to Parliament Reviewing the Provisions and Operation of the Federal Child Support Guidelines
http://canada.justice.gc.ca/en/ps/sup/pub/rp/volume_2_toc.html
A review of child support laws and practices in Canada.

Fathers, Marriage, and the Next Phase of Welfare Reform
http://www.acton.org/ppolicy/forum/no3.html
Though American based, this article offers a different perspective on the father's traditional role of breadwinner.

Gay, Lesbian, Bisexual and Transgendered Resources
http://www.pridenet.com/family.html
The purpose of this website is to provide a "G-Rated," intense resource centre for gays and lesbians, as well as a focus on transgender and bisexual resources.

Solutions

True or False?

1. T
2. T
3. F
4. T
5. F
6. T
7. F
8. T
9. F
10. T

Multiple Choice

1. D
2. C
3. D
4. C
5. B
6. C
7. D
8. C
9. B
10. D
11. B
12. A

13. B
14. D
15. C

Chapter 13

Work and Occupations

Chapter Introduction

I'm laughing as I type this, just thinking about all the crazy jobs that I've done over the years in order to make money to pay my tuition. You couldn't pay me enough to go back to work at a factory. I did two summers working on the assembly line at General Motors and on some days I think that I still smell like auto parts. What became very clear to me during those summers is that there is a huge gender gap in much of the work that is done in today's society — female summer students were definitely treated differently from male summer students and all summer students were treated differently from all permanent workers. I also learned a very valuable lesson during that time — that I won't do a job that I don't like, regardless of the salary that I can earn. I am certainly not saying that this should apply to anyone other than me, but I think that it is important to determine these kinds of job characteristics before you actually start training for a career. This past term I asked my students how many of them would shovel manure if it paid a lot of money. They wanted qualification on exactly what "a lot of money" meant and I told them that the job would consist of eight hour shifts, with breaks and would pay an hourly wage of $78.00. What do you think the reaction was? Would you take this job? OK, I won't hold you in suspense. I was actually surprised by the results. At first, literally every student indicated that they would take on this job, but when we discussed the actual work, many changed their answers. I have learned the hard way that, once again, life is too long to be doing a job you don't like. I suspect that those students who said that they'd shovel manure for the rest of their lives might just end up doing that. The others will most likely invest in their education and not have to worry about falling in a pile of manure and coming up smelling like a rose.

In this chapter, you'll learn what the service economy means for our working lives, how employees and employers do battle to gain the upper hand in determining what jobs will be like, what factors lead to "good jobs" or "bad jobs," and if these jobs will be satisfying to workers.

The study of work and occupations is a study of both the constraints and the struggles that happen every day in Canadian workplaces.

Learning Objectives

At the conclusion of this chapter, you should be able to discuss or write about the following, without having to rely on the textbook:

1. In the first industrial revolution, large segments of the population moved from being peasant farmers to being wage-earning factory workers living in urban areas. During the second revolution, companies increased in size and developed administrative offices with a complex division of labour.

2. The rise of the service economy is changing the types of jobs available in the labour market. The types of jobs in the service economy are being polarized into good jobs in upper-tier industries and bad jobs in lower-tier industries.

3. The proportion of Canadians employed in nonstandard jobs is growing. Much of this job growth is fuelled by the expansion of the lower-tier service sector.

4. Labour-market segmentation shows that different segments exist in the labour market. Good jobs are located in core industries and firms with secondary labour markets. Job ghettos are areas of the labour market that trap disadvantaged groups of workers. Labour-market shelters, such as professional associations and unions, help their members maintain access to good jobs.

5. From Taylorism to the Japanese management, various management strategies are used to control workers and increase their productivity. Most strategies fall short on their claims to be participatory.

6. Research does not show a difference in men and women's management styles. Differences are due to the position of managers or their organizational context.

7. Job satisfaction measures how workers feel about their jobs. Work and organizational characteristics are the primary predictors of how satisfied workers are.

8. Alienation is a structural condition of powerlessness that arises from the organization of work in the capitalist economy. Workers respond to alienating conditions in various ways, such as engaging in sabotage or quitting their jobs. Strikes and other collective forms of resistance may have some success in changing the conditions of work.

Quiz Questions

True or False?

1. Hiring disabled workers is not as costly as some employers believe. Recent studies show that only 20 percent of people with disabilities require changes to the physical accommodations of workplaces in order to work.
    True or False

2. By breaking jobs into their smallest components and removing the need for workers to think, Taylorism opened the door for management to reduce their reliance on skilled labour.
    True or False

3. The labour-market-segmentation theory suggests that regardless of where you enter the labour market, there is always an opportunity for getting a different, better-paying job.
    True or False

4. Job ghettos are parts of the labour market that trap certain groups of workers. Structural barriers based on stereotypes work to keep some of the individuals from entering the primary labour market and the best jobs.
    True or False

5. Although some technological determinists might have us believe that the implementation of technology in our workplaces is an inevitable process, most sociologists view the effects of technology as contingent on various economic and technological factors.
    True or False

6. The consensus that seems to be growing among researchers is that no real differences exist between male and female managerial behaviour and effectiveness. This body of research

suggests, that rather than defining certain managerial styles as male and female, we should develop a contextualized understanding of managerial styles.
True or False

7. In the early nineteenth century, the second industrial revolution started. This revolution included the rise of consolidated companies, where large companies brought up smaller companies engaged in similar types of production, in such industries as steel and railroads.
True or False

8. Secondary labour-market jobs do not offer much of a job ladder. These jobs are sometimes referred to as "dead-end jobs" because of their lack of upward mobility.
True or False

9. "Hawthorne studies" started the movement to consider how employers can fulfill employees' social needs, increase their satisfaction, and make them feel better about their jobs.
True or False

10. Work in Canada is dominated by the knowledge sector: Jobs are becoming polarized into good and bad jobs, and nonstandard or part-time jobs are becoming more prevalent.
True or False

Multiple Choice

1. At minimum, good jobs are those that provide _____ rewards, such as good wages, benefits, employment security, and opportunities for advancement.

   a. intrinsic

   b. extrinsic

   c. merit based

   d. annual

2. While _____ was geared toward removing the need for workers to think on the job, more recent strategies have paid more attention to the ability and desire of workers to participate in workplace decisions.

   a. Japanese technology

   b. the division of labour

   c. Taylorism

   d. team work

3. The growing number of part-time workers who would prefer full-time work is disturbing. In most industrial countries, including Canada, approximately _____ of all jobs are now nonstandard.

   a. one-eighth to one-quarter

   b. one-quarter

   c. one-quarter to one-third

   d. one-half

4. In Canada between 1971 and 1991, the number of women managers increased from 6 percent to 38 percent of all managers. However, since roughly _____ percent of senior managers in Canada are women, the "glass ceiling" for women has by no means disappeared.
   a. 21
   b. 25
   c. 30
   d. 35

5. In order to respond to changes in demand for their products and services, some employers now rely on temporary workers, ranging from clerical help to computer programmers, hired through temporary employment agencies. Like part-time workers, temporaries tend to be _____
   a. young and male.
   b. young and female.
   c. visible minorities.
   d. retired women.

6. Good jobs should provide _____ rewards such as decision-making opportunities, challenging non-repetitive work, and autonomy that allows for self-direction and responsibility over work tasks.
   a. intrinsic
   b. extrinsic
   c. merit-based
   d. annual

7. Early studies of professions attempted to delineate their general characteristics or hallmarks. Which of the following is not one of them?
   a. All professional occupations control a special body of abstract knowledge.
   b. Professional occupations are autonomous.
   c. Professional occupations deserve higher wages.
   d. Professionals generally have authority over their clients and subordinates.

8. Although we still see vestiges of the first and second industrial revolutions in our working lives, many things have changed. Most prominent is the movement away from a manufacturing-based economy toward a _____ economy.
   a. service
   b. technological
   c. knowledge
   d. agrarian

9. In looking at the ten most common jobs for men and women, the 1996 census shows that _____ jobs dominate for both sexes.
   a. teaching
   b. administrative
   c. health related
   d. retail service

10. _____ are parts of the labour market that trap certain groups of workers.

    a. Primary labour markets

    b. Job ghettos

    c. Secondary labour markets

    d. Dead-end jobs

11. In order to respond to changes in demand for their products and services, some employers now rely on temporary workers, ranging from clerical help to computer programmers, hired through temporary-employment agencies. In 2001, almost _____ of Canadian workers were employed in temporary or contract positions.

    a. 8%

    b. 13%

    c. 18%

    d. 23%

12. Organizations now talk about managing diversity within their boundaries. This is the catchphrase for programs designed to reduce barriers for women, visible minorities, Aboriginal people, and people with disabilities. Which of the following is not an effective tool for managing diversity?

    a. creating voluntary overtime packages

    b. sexual harassment awareness seminars

    c. hiring and promoting visible minorities

    d. establishing mentor relationships

13. According to Max Weber, bureaucracies are the most efficient and rational organization form for reaching the goals of capitalism. Which of the following is not characteristic of bureaucracies?

    a. Written rules provide guidelines for handling routine situations.

    b. A complex division of labour ensures that workers know what is required of them and helps to identify who is responsible for when something goes wrong.

    c. Bureaucracies are a way to overcome arbitrary decisions and corruption in non-bureaucratic organizations.

    d. Bureaucracies experience increased profits because of reduced overhead costs.

14. Unions play an important role in facilitating collective action by workers but are still faced with difficulties in organizing women. Over the past 20 years, the number of women in unions has increased; in 1990, women accounted for _____ of all union memberships.

    a. 18%

    b. 27%

    c. 43%

    d. 52%

15. How do Canadians feel about their jobs? According to a 2001 survey, _____ of Canadians reported that they were satisfied with their jobs.
    a. 26%
    b. 45%
    c. 74%
    d. 93%

Critical Thinking

1. The story of Debora De Angelis that begins this chapter strikes a chord of familiarity with me. Having to depend on a variety of part-time and sessional teaching positions to finance my education, I know all too well the differences that exist between full-time employees and part-time or contractual help. Do you find yourself in the same situation as Debora? Are you overworked in an underpaid environment? Quitting a job is a big decision, especially when your job is one that allows you to earn some money while you're in school. What can you do to improve your situation? Would you support a union? Why or why not?

2. Thinking back to my summers at GM, I remember that, at the time, the economy was good and the company offered full-time positions to summer students. I remember my supervisor asking me if I'd like to stay on and I vividly remember my response. I told him, "I'd rather eat a bug." There was not enough money in the world to make me stay on. Would you take on a job that you know you wouldn't like just because the money is good? How long do you think that you would last at it? Is there a job that you wouldn't do, regardless of the pay?

3. Until recently, only doctors had the authority to deliver babies. Doctors maintained their authority because of their monopoly over the relevant body of knowledge and used their national associations to lobby provincial and federal governments to deny others the right to practise medicine. As a result of current public demands for access to midwives and the development of professional midwifery schools, doctors have lost some control over the birthing process and have lost their monopoly over this body of professional knowledge. What do you think of this? Should midwives be covered by the same provincial medical insurance as doctors? What about those much-needed medical professionals like chiropractors or naturopaths that seem to fall between the cracks. How would you decide the membership of a professional organization?

4. In this chapter, the author mentions the commercial for Saturn vehicles. The commercial was about an employee who noticed a problem in assembly and "stopped the line." The commercial emphasized the fact that this employee stopped the line to correct what would ultimately end up being a defect in the car. Why do you think this action was the focus of the commercial? As a consumer, wouldn't you expect the product to be built properly before it left the factory, regardless of who stopped the line or how often? Does this lead you to believe that other car companies hire employees who don't care about their work? Do you think that Saturn has an effective advertising campaign?

Web Links

McJobberTakes Back Her Future
http://www.web.net/~ondp/nod/dec97/mcjobber.htm
This website provides additional information on Debora De Angelis.

National Occupational Classification 2001 — Welcome
http://www23.hrdc-drhc.gc.ca/2001/e/generic/welcome.shtml
Since its introduction in 1992, the National Occupational Classification system continues to be the authoritative resource on occupational information in Canada.

JobFutures
http://www.jobfutures.ca/en/home.shtml
Use this website to discover how likely you are to succeed in the career of your choice.

Welcome to Labour Market Information
http://lmi-imt.hrdc-drhc.gc.ca/
Answer your questions about jobs, skills, and worker availability in local areas across Canada.

Centre for the Study of Education and Work
http://www1.oise.utoronto.ca/research/wall/people_partners/investigators.htm
This is a website that describes the work I'm doing for my doctoral degree. Look for my name to learn more about me!

Solutions

True or False?

1. T
2. T
3. F
4. T
5. F
6. T
7. F
8. T
9. T
10. F

Multiple Choice

1. B
2. C
3. C
4. A
5. B
6. A
7. C
8. A
9. D
10. B
11. B
12. A
13. D
14. C
15. D

Chapter 14

Education

Chapter Introduction

If you've read the bio piece on me in the front of your study guide, you'll know that I fit the bill for what my family calls, a "professional student." I prefer to refer to myself as a life-long learner and can't imagine my life without being involved in some form of education. I'm not exactly sure why I'm addicted to learning, especially when no one else in my family is, but I do know that it has nothing to do with the money that I might earn in my career. Are your educational plans directly related to the type of career that you're planning to enter? How much formal education will your job require? What's the best thing about being a student? What are the parts that you don't like very much? These should be the best years of your life, if you can find the perfect balance between going to school and having fun. It works best if you can go to school and have fun at the same time. I don't really have a personal philosophy but I've always believed that school should never have to hurt — if it does, then you're doing something wrong. Oftentimes that just means tweaking your schedule or cutting down back on the hours that you spend at a part-time job, but you should be able graduate with a smile on your face and be proud of your accomplishments while you look forward to using your skills in the workforce.

In this chapter, you'll explore how sociological theory and research can shed light on the operation of schools in a modern industrial society such as Canada. You'll learn about the critical importance of education both to individuals and to all of society. Three major sociological perspectives are examined, and the author shares the insight that these explanatory frameworks have provided historically and contemporarily. Additionally, this chapter is full of results from some very interesting research based on these perspectives that pertains to the operation of schools and the effectiveness of Canadian education.

Learning Objectives

At the conclusion of this chapter, you should be able to discuss or write about the following, without having to rely on the textbook:

1. Sociologists study education for several reasons. Educational attainment is linked to entry into the labour force, and affects both life-chances and quality of life. Effective mass education in Canada is a national priority. It is widely believed to play an important role in maintaining democratic ideals, equality, social justice, and economic productivity. Schooling is broadly considered to be an appropriate means of solving a wide variety of social problems including poverty, discrimination, crime, and illness.

2. Structural-functionalism presents education as a part of, and contributing to, a larger social system. It emphasizes equilibrium, value consensus, and gradual social change.

3. Manifest (or intended) functions include personal development, cultural transmission, and the creation, preservation, and dissemination of knowledge. Latent (or unintended) functions include providing a marriage market, legitimizing social inequity, and restricting competition for jobs.

4. Conflict theories of education are based on the work of Max Weber and Karl Marx. They emphasize disagreements and power struggles in educational contexts, particularly along the lines of class, ethnicity, and gender.

5. Marxist conflict theory analyzes schooling as a tool of the capitalist elite and as a generator of working class resistance.

6. Weberian conflict theory presents the argument that schooling is a means of bestowing credentials.

7. Symbolic interaction is an interpretive framework that focuses on the development of self-image, self-concept, or identity. Interactionists view a person's self-concept as the product of the manipulation and interpretation of symbols in long-term social interaction. Over time, people develop positive or negative senses of self in response to the perceived reactions of significant others who surround them.

8. Out of the meanings arising from interaction, people construct three important definitions that greatly affect their current and future actions — self, society, and situation. Each of these definitions significantly influences subsequent behaviour, including behaviour in school and educational outcomes.

9. Evidence suggests that student characteristics are correlated with educational outcomes and that equality of opportunity is not the same as equality in results. Students from lower-class and some ethnic backgrounds (e.g., Aboriginal) do not do as well in school as students from higher-class and other ethnic backgrounds (e.g., Jewish and Asian).

10. Female students perform as well or better than male students. Although differences between male and female participation rates in postsecondary education have disappeared in recent years, important differences remain with respect to particular programs.

11. Student outcomes are affected by the interaction of personal traits, home environment, and school experiences. Key elements of the home that affect schooling are language use and access to cultural capital. Important elements of the school experience include teacher expectations, tracking, and the informal (or hidden) curriculum.

Quiz Questions

True or False?

1. The formal curriculum in school encourages students' acceptance of authority and social control. In addition to the transmission of knowledge, it teaches today's students (who will be tomorrow's workers) to line up, follow directions, and respect authority.
    True or False

2. On the individual level, education largely determines a person's social status and quality of life through its impact on occupation, income, and prestige. More years in school generally translate to greater labour-force participation, higher income, and lower unemployment.
    True or False

3. Historically, Canadian research has consistently shown a wide disparity between males and females when it comes to quantitative measures of educational aspirations and high-school completion rates. This pattern has held regardless of students' socioeconomic backgrounds.
    True or False

4. There are two fundamental reasons why employers demand credentials despite the fact that content of many lines of work has remained much the same over time. First, selection on the basis of certification represents a solution to the problems posed by an oversupply of capable workers. Secondly, despite of the lack of solid evidence, it is widely believed that workers with more education are more productive.
   True or False

5. At the elementary and secondary levels, males and females are enrolled in roughly equal numbers. Males are better readers, communicate more effectively, get higher grades, fail fewer subjects, and are less likely to drop out.
   True or False

6. Historically, research has unearthed biases in teachers' lessons and the information presented in instructional materials. There is evidence of some change, but both teachers and texts, especially at the elementary rather than secondary levels, present the ideals rather than the realities of everyday living.
   True or False

7. Doing well in school is not just a matter of intelligence; students' social characteristics such as gender, ethnicity, and socioeconomic status affect educational attainment.
   True or False

8. Guppy and Davis (1998) examined salaries by education level and found that someone with a bachelor's degree earned a yearly salary almost $15 000 higher than a high school drop out.
   True or False

9. High-status or elite families provide their children with a lot of what Bourdieu (1973) calls "human capital." Human capital accumulates through exposure in the home to fine art, classical music, ballet, opera, and the great books. This exposure encourages people to define themselves as "cultured" and definition fosters in children strong self-concepts that are valuable assets in the educational process.
   True or False

10. Evidence shows that women's self-concept causes them to prefer learning that allows for the expression of qualities such as caring for others and reciprocity. Success in science, by contrast, has traditionally involved the expression of masculine qualities of autonomy and limited cooperative learning.
    True or False

Multiple Choice

1. Tracking, streaming, or ability grouping has been a hotly debated practice for decades. More than _____ of parents and teachers in Ontario support some form of streaming and a third of both groups support tracking at or before Grade 9.
   a. 60%
   b. 70%
   c. 80%
   d. 90%

2. The average Black student still scores below 75% of whites on most standardized tests. In the last decade, a 17-year-old Black demonstrated an average proficiency in reading, writing, science, and math roughly equivalent to a _____ white.

   a. 12-year-old

   b. 13-year-old

   c. 14-year-old

   d. 15-year-old

3. According to _____, learning orderly conduct, punctuality, obedience, and loyalty to the prevailing political and economic system helps young people fit their future roles as employees in industry and commerce.

   a. Mink and Evans

   b. Marx and Durkheim

   c. Bowles and Gintis

   d. Weber and Guppy

4. Out of the meanings arising from social interaction, people construct three important definitions that greatly affect their current and future actions. Which of the following is not one of them?

   a. self

   b. society

   c. situation

   d. solution

5. Segregation by sex in college and university program participation and graduation is of considerable significance for several reasons. Which of the following is not one of them?

   a. Some programs offer greater certainty of labour-force entry opportunities.

   b. Most employment opportunities in traditionally male-dominated occupations do not allow for the disruption of service due to pregnancy.

   c. Training in some fields leads to jobs with higher levels of remuneration.

   d. Sex segregation in the world of work means there is a narrower range of jobs for which women can compete in practice.

6. Education is a vital concern to ethnic groups in three ways. Which of the following is not one of them?

   a. The increase in credentialed visible minorities has prompted employers to institute the formation of affirmative action programs.

   b. Education can offer access to better-paying jobs and upward social and economic mobility.

   c. Education can be a means of providing or strengthening a collective sense of self and group identity.

   d. Education can be an effective means of reducing prejudice and discrimination.

7. A nation's economic productivity in an age of industrialization and technological development requires a highly skilled and knowledgeable labour force. A highly effective education system is indispensable to the creation of _____ that will facilitate and stimulate economic productivity as Canada competes with other developed nations for increasingly mobile investment dollars.

   a. "human capital"

   b. "cultural capital"

   c. "overhead capital"

   d. "diversified capital"

8. _____ argue that education, like other social institutions, operates to satisfy several needs that must be met if society is to survive and prosper. For example, the growth of mass education is held to be a direct response to the skill and knowledge requirements of industrial society.

   a. Progressive education theorists

   b. Functionalists

   c. Conflict theorists

   d. Symbolic interactionists

9. In an Ontario Institute for Studies in Education survey, the percentage of respondents who believe that public education is improving dropped from more than 35% in 1979 to less than 20% in 2001. In part, the public's response has been to abandon the public system entirely and pursue alternatives; an estimated _____ families across Canada home-schooled their children in 2001.

   a. 40 000

   b. 60 000

   c. 80 000

   d. 100 000

10. Which of the following is not a version of conflict theory, as it attempts to explain education?

   a. Education as a capitalist tool

   b. Resistance theory

   c. Economic discrepancy theory

   d. Credentialism

11. Researchers advocate providing more resources to facilitate learning for students in lower-track environments. To solve the attainment deficits inherent in lower-track assignment, they also recommend_____

   a. segregating classes by gender.

   b. mixing students of differing abilities.

   c. hiring more educational assistants.

   d. extra-curricular tutoring.

12. Open education maximizes student-centred approaches while minimizing relationships based on authority. It relaxes rules and diversifies the curriculum in nontraditional areas. Students set their own goals, learn at their own pace, and are evaluated without the use of grades. Nonetheless, criticism of open education was intense, and commentators have agreed that, overall, the educational reforms of the _____ ended in failure.

    a. 1940s

    b. 1950s

    c. 1960s

    d. 1970s

13. College instructors and university professors enjoy higher status, more prestige, and more power than secondary school teachers for several reasons. Which of the following is not one of them?

    a. They have more advanced educational qualifications.

    b. They produce knowledge as well as transmit it.

    c. The ability to gain tenure offers job security.

    d. Their teaching activity involves presenting sophisticated arguments and original analyses to a clientele comprised of adults.

14. _____ is a micro-level framework that focuses on understanding the processes involved in social learning. As an interpretive perspective, it explores how people develop identities and self-concepts and how these in turn affect behaviour.

    a. Functionalism

    b. Progressive education theory

    c. Symbolic interactionism

    d. Transformative education theory

15. In their analyses of the 1994 General Social Survey, Guppy and Davies (1998) found that _____ young men and women whose fathers were in the professional-managerial group were likely to have studied at the university level. By comparison, those whose fathers were farmers or unskilled labourers were much less likely to have done so.

    a. one in ten

    b. three in ten

    c. five in ten

    d. six in ten

Critical Thinking

1. *Maclean's* magazine cites two polls conducted in 2001 suggesting that the public confidence in Canada's school system is middling at best. In a Gallup poll, less than half the respondents claimed satisfaction with the education of Canadian children. The response of the provincial governments has been to adopt market-oriented bureaucratic solutions. Mike Harris's Conservative government introduced measures aimed at increasing accountability and tightening bureaucratic control. The government's initiatives called for a common curriculum, standardized testing, and uniform report cards for students, as well as compulsory testing and professional upgrading for teachers. What do you think of these initiatives? What problems

with the system do you think that they address? How successful will they be, and how do you think that levels of success will be measured?

2. Market critics of contemporary education point out that education is both an essential service and a monopoly. Essential and without competitors, critics argue that the system is overly autonomous, unresponsive, and resistant to change. Advocates of market-based reform strategies maintain that school choice would breed competition, greatly improve responsiveness and accountability, and thereby enhance the quality of education. If schools were allowed to compete for students, do you feel that it would affect the quality of education? What are the advantages or disadvantages of open competition for school? How would you measure an institution's level of success?

3. Jobs that once called for only an elementary or secondary school diploma now require a university degree, and jobs that once required an undergraduate degree now call for a graduate or professional degree. Instead of an increasingly complex society that demands more sophisticated skills in the workplace, jobs are deskilled by technology, and access to good jobs is controlled by credentials that bear little relation to skill. There is an assumption that most people can do most jobs and learn them in a short time at work. Do you agree or disagree with this theory? How does this make you feel about your own schooling?

4. Until the late 1960s students in secondary schools were clearly streamed into vocational or academic programs, each with its own course requirements, examinations, and diplomas. The academic track included those bound for postsecondary education, while educators reserved the terminal track for those whose dismal academic performance marked them for unskilled jobs or unemployment. Students from working-class homes were more likely to be in the vocational stream; girls were more likely to be in the typing classes; children from most ethnic minorities were more likely to be in the lower academic streams. Does streaming still exist today, even covertly? Is it related in any way to the double cohort in Ontario? Are high schools preparing students for further education or to enter a workforce that is becoming increasingly reliant on knowledge and skills?

Web Links

Indian and Northern Affairs Canada
http://www.ainc-inac.gc.ca/ps/edu/index_e.html
An objective view of the relationship between Aboriginals and higher education in Canada, including job links.

Human Capital Cluster Group — Environment and Sustainable Development Indicators
http://www.nrtee-trnee.ca/eng/programs/Current_Programs/SDIndicators/ClusterGroups/
Human_Capital_e.htm
Here is an abundance of information on one of my favourite theories.

History of Education: How Schools Structure Inequality
http://fcis.oise.utoronto.ca/~daniel_schugurensky/assignment1/1985oakes.html
This website details the historical roots and perpetuation of inequality in education in Canada.

Higher Education Search Engines
http://www.searchengineguide.com/pages/Education/Higher_Education/
This website is an excellent resource to assist you in researching on the Internet, especially in
the area of education.

Solutions

True or False?

1. F
2. T
3. F
4. T
5. F
6. T
7. T
8. F
9. T
10. T

13. C
14. C
15. D

Multiple Choice

1. D
2. B
3. C
4. D
5. B
6. A
7. A
8. B
9. C
10. C
11. B
12. C

Chapter 15

Urbanization

Chapter Introduction

I remember my very first trip to Toronto. I was about 12 years old and I can still remember the overwhelming feeling that I got when I saw a homeless man for the first time in my life. It was devastating for me and more than a bit confusing. I had no idea that homeless people even existed. I remember giving him all the money that I had to spend (which wasn't much) and walking away feeling totally inadequate. We didn't have homeless people in the city where I grew up, so seeing the poverty that existed in a city that wasn't so far away from home really opened my eyes to what was going on in the world. I quickly became more aware of the differences between urban and rural life and for a while I tended to blame homelessness on the city planners for not having the foresight to see that what they were building was not really affordable housing for a large segment of the population. I've since learned that homelessness is about much more than the physical structures that define a society and I now know that it can be explained by the social institutions and relations that exist in our world. Just knowing about this is hardly enough to eliminate it, but I think that the greatest place to initiate change is in our minds and hearts. I think that, by now, you should have a greater understanding of how difficult it is to make any changes in society, and the bigger the issue that you want to change, the more resources you need to make it happen.

In this chapter you'll learn about the dual influence of environment and structure on city life over the course of the twentieth century. You'll also come to understand that there are three main types of cities: the industrial city, the corporate city, and the postmodern city.

Learning Objectives

At the conclusion of this chapter, you should be able to discuss or write about the following, without having to rely on the textbook:

1. Cities are defined as relatively large, dense, permanent settlements in which the majority of residents do not produce their own food.

2. Until the Industrial Revolution, cities were incapable of supporting more than about 5% of the total societal population, largely because of the absence of agricultural surpluses great enough to feed a huge urban population.

3. The best-known urban growth model in the social sciences is Ernest Burgess's concentric-zone scheme in which the expansion of cities is conceptualized as a successive series of rings and circles, each of which segregates a distinct resident population and type of land use. Other more recent explanations favour patterns of urban growth resembling pie-shaped wedges that develop along transportation routes or multiple nodes of economic activity, each with its own nucleus.

4. In contrast to the rise of the city in Western Europe and North America, cities of the South have grown at a much faster rate than the industrial economy. The resulting "over-urbanization" has accelerated problems of poverty and unemployment, which are rooted in basic structural inequalities and uneven development.

5. The corporate city of the 1950s and 1960s was the product of an urban-growth machine in which a coalition of politicians, planners, real-estate developers, business people, and other interest groups joined forces in order to engineer economic development and progress. The main products of this alliance were (a) the corporate suburbs, (b) shopping centres, (c) suburban industrial parks, (d) downtown office towers, and (e) high-rise apartment buildings.

6. Three alternative theories — structural, selective migration, and class life and life-cycle stage — have been proposed to explain the relationship between suburban residence and lifestyle patterns. Although all these theories have merit, the suburban way of life observed by many researchers in the 1950s and 1960s appears to have been a unique product of a particular time and place.

7. In recent decades, the contemporary city has mirrored and incorporated a bifurcated global economy. On the one hand, there is an upper-tier informational city whose members work in jobs related to financial services, telecommunications, and high technology and either live in gentrified downtown neighbourhoods or in private communities on the edge of the city. Together, the informational city and the informal economy constitute the dual city whose residents have little in common with each other.

8. One of the defining characteristics of the postmodern city is the increasing privatization of public spaces. This is manifested in three ways: (a) the growth of private enclosed places, such as malls, festival market places, and themed entertainment complexes, that offer pale imitations of urbanity; (b) the booming growth of gated communities and other private residential enclaves where outsiders are not welcome; and (c) the construction of fortress cities where tourists and other affluent consumers are kept in while the homeless and the urban poor are kept out.

Quiz Questions

True or False?

1. In the latter part of the nineteenth century, the German philosopher George Simmel attempted to depict the difference between traditional and modern societies by introducing the difference between *Gemeischaft* and *Gesellschaft*. He used them to describe the community of feeling that exists in villages and small communities.
   True or False

2. Not all of us get to choose our community freely, but people will always strive to match their choices with their needs. The environmental-opportunity theory posits that people actively choose where they want to live depending on the extent to which a particular place either meshes with or constrains their preferred lifestyle.
   True or False

3. Chauncey Harris and Edward Ullman (1945) proposed a multiple-nuclei model of urban growth in which were located a series of growth centres — retail, wholesale, residential — each representing the concentration of a specific function or activity within the urban economy.
   True or False

4. A century ago, most urban growth was concentrated in the rapidly industrializing countries of Europe and North America. Today, nearly two-thirds of the world's urban population resides in less developed regions of Asia, Oceania, Africa, Latin America, and the Caribbean.
   True or False

5. To a greater extent than with Northern cities, cities of the South are characterized by a high degree of overpopulation. Overpopulation describes a situation where one metropolitan centre is significantly larger and more dominant than any of the others.
   True or False

6. Berger (1960) defines the myth of suburbia as a standardized and stereotyped view of the suburbs as uniformly middle-class, homogeneous, conformist, child-centred, female-dominated hotbeds of sociability.
   True or False

7. Gentrification refers to the transformation of working-class housing into fashionable downtown neighbourhoods by middle- and upper-income newcomers. Gentrification was neither anticipated nor accounted for by earlier ecological growth models.
   True or False

8. In a much cited before — after study of middle-class couples in Toronto who chose to relocate during the early 1970s, Michaelson (1973) found that suburban movers decreased their involvement with neighbours, while city re-locators increased interactions with friends and relatives.
   True or False

9. In the United States, nearly 4 million residents are estimated to live in closed-off, gated communities, and another 28 million in areas governed by private community associations. This makes private communities the fastest-growing residential communities in the U.S.
   True or False

10. The fortress city is a city of simulations. That is, urban cityscapes are deliberately constructed so as to replicate reality, but without any of the warts to be found in the original.
    True or False

Multiple Choice

1. Three elements of prime importance characterized pre-industrial cities. Which of the following is not one of them?
   a. the existence of food surplus in fertile valleys, which permitted the specialization of labour in zones of dense settlement
   b. an autocratic system of government that oversaw the health and wealth of the populace
   c. the achievement of literacy among scribes, priests, and other elite members of society, which allowed for the keeping of financial and other records
   d. technological innovations, notably metallurgy, agricultural irrigation, and the harnessing of wind and water power for sailing and grain milling

2. As the twentieth century progressed, the proportion of the Canadian population that was classified as "urban" increased dramatically, reaching _____ in 1951. By 1991, 77% of the Canadian population was living in towns and cities.
   a. 35%
   b. 45%
   c. 55%
   d. 70%

3. By the final quarter of the nineteenth century, U.S. cities were seeing jumps in the population that rivalled and even surpassed those in Britain. Nowhere was this more dramatic than in _____, which mushroomed from 122 000 people in 1860 to 1.7 million in 1900.

   a. Chicago

   b. New York

   c. Seattle

   d. Houston

4. The spatial logic of the edge city dictates that centres and boundaries are not needed. Instead, the edge city is made up of three overlapping types of socioeconomic networks. Which of the following is not one of them?

   a. household networks

   b. networks of consumption

   c. networks of production

   d. networks of communication

5. In the early 1950s _____, Canada's first mass suburb, was built on the northern fringe of Toronto.

   a. Scarborough

   b. Don Mills

   c. Mississauga

   d. York

6. Burgess's concentric zone model made three interrelated assumptions. Which of the following is not one of them?

   a. Zones would eventually become integrated, leading to massive urban centres.

   b. All commercial growth was said to emanate from the dominant city-centre nucleus and proceeds outward in an orderly and predictable manner.

   c. Residential growth took place at the periphery, where it was easier and cheaper to obtain open land for development purchases.

   d. The model was dynamic, in that it assumed a sort of filtering-down process.

7. By the end of the _____ century, a brand-new type of city had begun to emerge, first in England and later in continental Europe and America. This industrial city was larger, more complex, and more dynamic than any urban settlement that had preceded it.

   a. 16th

   b. 17th

   c. 18th

   d. 19th

8. Which of the following is not a theory that contributed to the explanation of the growth of industrial cities?

    a. a boom in trade and commerce, which provided a powerful inducement to greater investment, technological improvements and ultimately, increased agricultural production

    b. a shift in the sources of capital accumulation — that is, how factory owners raised the investment money needed to build and improve their manufacturing facilities.

    c. the invention of the factory, allowing work to be done in villages instead of at home

    d. an increase in agricultural sustainability, allowing men to work in factories while women and children worked at home

9. At the time of Confederation in 1867, Canada lagged significantly behind both Britain and the United States in the development of an urban-industrial economy. Through various interventions by the federal government, a system of national economic markets was eventually established. Which of the following is not one of the interventions?

    a. the design and construction of locks on the St. Lawrence Seaway

    b. the building of the transcontinental railroad

    c. the imposition of a protective tariff system to encourage domestic manufacturing

    d. a vigorous immigration policy that encouraged agriculture on the Prairies

10. Burgess's urban-growth model appears to have fit Chicago reasonably well, but as a scheme for understanding all cities in different places and times it does not do as well. Which of the following is not a critique of Burgess's model?

    a. The notion of a single growth nucleus has not held up very firmly.

    b. Burgess seems to have underestimated the importance of transportation corridors as magnets for urban growth.

    c. He failed to appreciate that some resident groups would develop strong residential attachments to their neighbourhoods and refuse to move on, even in the face of an aging housing stock.

    d. Burgess didn't foresee the fluctuation in value of the U.S. dollar and, consequently, could not meet construction costs.

11. First-generation postwar suburbs shared five main characteristics. Which of the following was not one of them?

    a. a peripheral location

    b. relatively high population densities

    c. low purchase prices for houses

    d. a fairly high degree of economic and racial homogeneity

12. As cities began to grow in medieval times, periodic outbreaks of the bubonic plague killed as many as half the people in Europe's cities. Thus, by 1800, of the roughly 900 million people in the world, only about _____ percent lived in urban places of 5000 or more inhabitants.

    a. 3

    b. 5

    c. 8

    d. 11

13. The concept of _____ has provoked considerable debate among social scientists. Some claim that it is the single most important factor leading to the generation and intensification of serious social problems in southern cities: grinding poverty, mass unemployment, inadequate services, social unrest, increasing crime, and political instability.

    a. urban bias

    b. peri-urbanization

    c. over-urbanization

    d. urban primacy

14. In Brazil, where there are notoriously poor slums in Rio de Janeiro and Sao Paulo, approximately _____ of the population in rural areas continues to live below the poverty line, compared to roughly 38% in the cities.

    a. 25%

    b. 55%

    c. 65%

    d. 78%

15. Louis Writh proposed that the city is characterized by the concurrent trends of increasing size, density, and heterogeneity. In his view, the city creates a distinct way of life — "urbanism" — that is economically efficient but socially destructive. Which of the following does not appear on Wirth's short list of urban characteristics?

    a. decline of the family

    b. the disappearance of the old neighbourhood

    c. the undermining of traditional bases of social solidarity

    d. an increasing reliance on technology for communication purposes

Critical Thinking

1. Does the life of Elinor Florence sound appealing to you? Do you think that you'd like to give up the hustle and bustle of the big city and move to somewhere with a slower pace of life, more leisure time, a greater sense of personal security, and no fast-food restaurants? If you're from a small town and suddenly find yourself amidst a whole new world at school, how do you deal with the "culture shock" that you're probably experiencing? On the other hand, if you already live in a big city, do you think that you could settle down in a small town? Will your views on this change once you've graduated and become settled in your chosen career? Where would you like to spend your retirement?

2. The fortress city, in which the urban disadvantaged are isolated socially and spatially from office workers, tourists, and suburban day-trippers sounds like an extreme example of city living, but this type of community is becoming more and more popular. These fortress cities remind me very much of the situation that I found myself in a few years back. I decided to treat myself to a much-needed vacation and went on one of those "all-inclusive" packages to the Dominican Republic. As long as I stayed on the highly guarded compound, I felt like I was living in paradise, but as soon as I walked outside the compound gates into the neighbouring village, it was a very different world. I felt somewhat guilty enjoying myself after seeing the poverty that

was just beyond the gate and I came back from my vacation more than a little unsettled. Have you ever found yourself in this situation or a similar one? What were your feelings?

3. Before World War II, North American cities such as Toronto were configured in a grid system, with residential avenues crossing long commercial streets at right angles. This spawned a lively "front-yard culture" in which passers-by regularly interacted with front porch sitters, since front yards and families faced the street rather than the house itself. I remember walking to the corner store with my mother when I was young and distinctly recall that the trip could sometimes take an hour or so, when the store was only five minutes away. We would stop and chat with all the neighbours that were out doing yard work, or just enjoying the summer sun. Is a trip to your corner store anything like that? Do you know the names of everyone that lives on your street? Do you think that it has more to do with the actual placement of the houses or more to do with changing values in today's society?

4. Located in the newer suburbs and in edge cities, private communities compete with central cities for residents, offering as incentives a homogenous middle-class population, physical security, stable housing values, local control and freedom from exposure to the social problems of the inner city. In the United States, nearly 4 million residents are estimated to live in closed-off, gated communities, and another 28 million in areas governed by private community associations. Gated communities seem to be the kind of thing that you only see in movies, but as you read in your text, they're becoming very popular. Would you live in a gated community? What would be the advantages and disadvantages of doing so? Would you change your opinion if you had children?

Web Links

Canada's Urbanization
http://www.sustreport.org/signals/canpop_urb.html
The Sustainability Reporting Program is Canada's first independent initiative to find out how we are doing at living in balance for the long term.

Toronto's Urban Region
http://www.clr.utoronto.ca/PROJECTS/Toronto/UN-GTA/un.intro.html
An up-close and personal view of the history and future of urbanization in Toronto.

Culture Shock
http://www.destineducation.ca/intstdnt/annex-e4_e.htm
This site offers a trendy new look at diversity in Canada and around the world. Lots of tips for coping with change.

Communities Project
http://www.lcc.gc.ca/en/themes/sr/cp/cp_main.asp
Sponsored by the Law Commission of Canada, this website provides recent information about community living and a host of related links.

Solutions

True or False?

1. F
2. T
3. T
4. T
5. F
6. T
7. F
8. F
9. T
10. F

Multiple Choice

1. B
2. D
3. A
4. D
5. B
6. A
7. C
8. D
9. A
10. D
11. B
12. A
13. C
14. C
15. D

Chapter 16

Sociology and the Environment

Chapter Introduction

Though I will admit that I should probably be more environmentally aware, I do try to use environment-friendly products and can honestly say that I've never littered in my life. I'm usually too busy to stop and appreciate the beauty that surrounds me, but last October I was driving home from a conference and I got lost. I ended up driving around for hours before I finally stopped and asked for directions. I would have stopped much sooner, but I was absolutely captured by the beauty of the leaves turning colour, and for the first time in far too long, I was really glad that I live in Canada. I suspect that it's much the same feeling that those who live close to the rain forests experience. I can't imagine the destruction of such beauty, yet it is occurring at an uncomfortably rapid pace. Try to take some time from your busy schedule to appreciate the wonders of nature that exist right outside your front door and imagine how you would feel if, one day, your favourite tree was gone and replaced by a communication tower. It's a very scary thing to think that our natural resources are being depleted, especially when you realize that it takes years for them to grow back. How often do you think about the environment that you live in? Do you recycle? Do your parents?

In this chapter you'll examine how sociology has dealt with global environmental awareness, concern, and actions. The author briefly outlines the traditional lack of concern with the environment in sociological theory and research and then examines the value conflict in contemporary societies. The value conflict exists between those who favour unlimited economic expansion and technological solutions to human problems and those who embrace a new "ecological" view of the world, in which nature is accorded a central place. You will also learn about four principal areas of sociological inquiry that relate to the environment. When you consider what an environmentally aware society we have become, you'll appreciate how much useful and thought-provoking information this chapter contains.

Learning Objectives

At the conclusion of this chapter, you should be able to discuss or write about the following, without having to rely on the textbook:

1. Sociological interest in the natural environment is quite recent, having first developed in the early 1970s. Sociology's reluctance to embrace the study of the environment reflects its heritage, wherein biology and nature were banished from the discipline in favour of socially based theories of behaviour.

2. A central focus for much of the sociological examination of the environment has been the deep-seated value cleavage between environmentalists and their opponents in industry and science. The latter support a dominant social paradigm that stresses materialism, economic growth, and the human right to dominate nature. In contrast, environmentalists propose an alternative environmental paradigm that emphasizes the need to adopt smaller-scale, decentralized economic and political structures that are in harmony with nature. This value-oriented environmentalism has

found its fullest expression in a number of "ecophilosophies" — deep ecology and ecofeminism — that have recently flourished on the margins of the environmental movement.

3. Support for environmentalism has remained remarkably constant for nearly 20 years. Although the majority of the population is generally supportive of environmental values, a young, well-educated, urban, liberal core has taken the lead in working for environmental change. Most other Canadians will recycle, purchase "green" products, and act positively toward the environment, but only to the extent that such action does not require any real sacrifice in terms of time and money.

4. In order to mobilize the reluctant majority, environmental-movement organizers develop frames (interpretations of events) that play up the possibility of an impending global collapse as a result of uncontrolled population growth and continued industrial growth. Global warming, expanding holes in the ozone layer, and the worldwide losses of biodiversity are the most recently identified symptoms of the impending crisis. The only solution, it is claimed, is to draw back and ease down, conserving resources, reducing pollution, and restricting population increase. However, these goals are especially difficult to achieve in the expanding economies of the Third World, where the environment is threatened by both unsustainable development and unsustainable impoverishment.

5. At the level of the local community, willingness to act on environmental problems rises as trust in expert institutions declines. This loss of trust is characteristic of neighbourhood-based environmental conflicts, in which citizens typically find the explanations and assurances offered by scientists and other authority figures to be faulty. Environmental-risk perception and action are also linked to people's participation in local social networks and community affairs.

6. The role of environmental entrepreneurs or claims-makers is vital in moving environmental issues from free-floating concerns to problems that are recognized and acted upon by those in power. These promoters, situated in science, environmental organizations, and the media, define problems such as acid rain, global warming, and ozone depletion; package them; and elevate them to action agendas.

7. The social construction of environmental problems does not occur in a vacuum but it is shaped by political and economic factors, to the extent that the powerful in society have the ability to act as gatekeepers, determining what is said and what is not relevant with respect to the environment. Environmental problems, then, are actively contested, often on the basis of acceptable or unacceptable risk. Social constructionism in the context of power inequality represents a promising sociological route to understanding the environment-society relationship.

Quiz Questions

True or False?

1. One focus of environmental sociology is the conflict between environmentalist and mainstream views. According to the mainstream view, people have the unalienable right to dominate nature, even if that involves polluting the environment.
    True or False

2. Environmental sociology is a rather new field, largely because Edward Park and the other founders of the field downplayed the role of biological and physical factors in influencing human affairs while at the same time elevating the importance of "social facts," such as norms, groups, and institutions.
    True or False

3. Critics of the Brundtland report point out that sustainable development requires an extraordinary degree of mutual cooperation and a deep commitment to reform, stating that this is difficult to achieve.
    True or False

4. After studying recycling behaviour across the province of Alberta, Dersken and Gartrell (1993) concluded that the key factor accounting for participation in recycling programs was the easy availability of curbside pickups rather than positive attitudes toward the environment.
    True or False

5. British sociologist Stephen Cotgrove (1982) lays out two conflicting paradigms concerning environmentalists. The alternative paradigm is anchored by the moral imperative of material-wealth creation and the moral conviction that humans have the inalienable right to dominate and harness the environment to that end.
    True or False

6. In addition to researching the social composition of the environmental movement, sociologists have also been interested in learning how environmentalists retaliate against the corporations that continue to destroy valuable natural resources.
    True or False

7. Deep ecologists believe that the relation of the individual to nature cannot be fully grasped intellectually but must ultimately be experienced directly. They regard science and scientists with a fair degree of suspicion, depicting them as being a part of the problem as much as a part of the solution.
    True or False

8. A central focus for many sociologists interested in the environment is the value cleavage between environmentalists and their opponents. At the core of the disagreement is the long-accepted notion that the environment is something to be actively used and exploited.
    True or False

9. In the first comprehensive review of the emergence of environmental sociology as a distinct area of inquiry, Dunlap and Catton (1979) distinguished between a "sociology of environmental issues" and "environmental sociology."
    True or False

10. The environmental-acceptance paradigm featured the ideals of steadily evolving social progress, increasing prosperity and material comfort, and class mobility for all segments of society. From this perspective, technology functioned as the linchpin of economic development, allowing humans to overcome the challenges presented by hostile habitats such as jungles, swamps, and deserts.
    True or False

Multiple Choice

1. The Brundtland report suggested that it is possible to have the best of both worlds:

    a. equitable compensation for useable natural resources

    b. mandatory repletion allotments that earn a decreased rate of interest

    c. continued economic growth, but not at the expense of the environment

    d. artificially grown products manufactured at reduced costs

2. Environmentalists such as _____ insist that the environmental dangers we face today are so extensive that we can survive as a species only to totally dismantling the "buzz saw of progress."

    a. David Suzuki

    b. Daniel Brown

    c. Dunlap and Cattan

    d. Luloff and Theodori

3. In the past, most sociologists shared the assumption of the general public that the world would see steady gains in material progress, fuelled by an apparently unlimited availability of natural resources such as coal, lumber, and water. From this perspective, technology functioned as the linchpin of economic development, allowing humans to overcome the challenges presented by hostile habitats such as jungles, swamps, and deserts. This _____ featured the ideals of steadily evolving social progress, increasing prosperity and material comfort, and class mobility for all segments of society.

    a. environmental adaptation thesis

    b. social growth theory

    c. human-exceptionalism paradigm

    d. utopian equality paradigm

4. Which of the following is not an area of theory and research that relates to the four principal areas of sociological inquiry relating to the environment.

    a. environmental attitudes, concern, and behaviour

    b. the link between environment and transnational corporations

    c. the political economy of the environment

    d. environmental risk and risk assessment

5. By the early _____, stimulated by increased societal attention to urban decay, pollution, overpopulation, resource shortages, and so on, a number of sociologists began at last to study environmental issues.

    a. 1950s

    b. 1960s

    c. 1970s

    d. 1980s

6. A central focus for many sociologists interested in the environment is the value cleavage between environmentalists and their opponents. Many of the key values that have governed North American life — activism, achievement, progress, pursuit of the good life, materialism — permit this orientation toward the environment. Environmentalists, in contrast, support a different value orientation, one that _____.

   a. advocates a more passive, less manipulative approach to nature

   b. is bold enough to place blame on the transnational corporations who destroy the environment

   c. calls for the union of nature and technology to an end that suits both

   d. suggests that the balance between nature and nurture needs adjusting

7. The Brundtland report defined _____ as "development that meets the needs of the present without compromising the ability of future generations to meet their own needs."

   a. environmental cooperation

   b. sustainable development

   c. equitable supply demand ration

   d. the green/greed debate

8. After studying recycling behaviour across the province of Alberta, Derksen and Gartrell (1993) concluded that the key factor accounting for participation in recycling programs was _____.

   a. the increase in respondents' environmental awareness

   b. the feeling that respondents' get from knowing that they're helping save the environment

   c. the ease with which respondents can dispose of their waste

   d. the easy availability of curbside pickups.

9. Researchers using U.S. data for the years 1973–1990 found that the level and social location of support for environmental protection have _____ for nearly 20 years.

   a. increased

   b. decreased

   c. remained stable

   d. not been properly measured

10. _____ promoted the economic-contingency hypothesis, which suggests that the broadening of the social bases of environmental concern depends on prevailing economic conditions.

   a. Buttel (1975)

   b. Binkus and Brown (1984)

   c. Jones and Dunlap (1992)

   d. David Suzuki (1977)

11. Do pro-environmental attitudes convert directly into environmentally friendly behaviour? Most studies have failed to make these linkages; however, Maloney and Ward (1973) have noted some observations. Which of the following is not one of them?
    a. People are more likely to actively support a cause that they can relate to on a personal level.
    b. Higher-class individuals are more likely to donate money to a worthy cause, rather than their time.
    c. Some individuals are hesitant to be openly supportive of environmental issues for fear of reprisal.
    d. People say they are willing to do a great deal to help curb pollution problems and are fairly emotional about it, but in fact they actually do very little and know even less.

12. In Canada, the conservation movement developed in a different fashion. Environmental initiatives, such as the establishment of national parks and the protection of wildlife, were more likely to be developed by small groups of _____ who were able to convince the federal government to take action.
    a. political activists
    b. university professors
    c. dedicated civil servants
    d. unemployed housewives

13. Contemporary environmental frames are frequently constructed around the image of an impending global collapse. In the early 1970s, this approach was typified by the best-selling book *The Limits to Growth* (Meadows et al., 1972), in which the authors forecast that earth's _____ — that is, the optimum population size that the planet can support under present environmental conditions — would eventually be exceeded.
    a. structural base
    b. population restriction
    c. explosion potential
    d. carrying capacity

14. History, as it has been taught in our schools, is an account of how the explorers, missionaries, traders, and industrialists rolled back the frontier, "tamed" nature, and brought prosperity to "virgin" lands. The great achievements of the last two centuries, except _____, all represent a triumph by science and industry over natural hazards and barriers.
    a. the Great Wall of China
    b. the opening of the Panama canal
    c. the completion of the Canadian transcontinental railway
    d. the landing of the astronauts on the moon

15. More recently, environmentalists have been identified as members of a "_____," drawn primarily from social and cultural specialists.
    a. more socially conscious class
    b. new intellectual class
    c. new middle class
    d. newly defined moral crusade

Critical Thinking

1. Greenbaum (1995) has characterized the social bases of environmental concern as "complex and subtle." That is because environmental concern spans a wide variety of subject matters, from species extinction and the thinning of the ozone layer to the contamination of local drinking waters by toxic chemicals. Although it may be possible to isolate general clusters of environmental concern, people may not be very consistent across various issues. Part of the reason for inconsistency is that individual environmental problems affect us in very different ways. With that in mind, do you think that environmental support could/should be measured on a continuum? Should there be varying levels of support? For example, what if you don't recycle, yet you support the preservation of the rain forests? Could your opinion be captured accurately by using a scale that is so rigid?

2. The authors of the best-selling book *Limits to Growth* (Meadows et al., 1972) forecast that the earth's carrying capacity — that is, the optimum population size that the planet can support under present environmental conditions — would eventually be exceeded. They predicted that, within a century, we would face a major crisis brought on by uncontrolled population growth and rising levels of pollution. What are your thoughts on this? Do you think that you would think or act differently when/if you have children? To what extent do you care about future generations?

3. The "biocentric" approach emphasizes that humans are one species among many on earth and have no special rights or privileges. This "biocentric egalitarianism" states that all things on earth have an equal right to live and blossom and reach their own forms of self-realization. Do you agree with this viewpoint? How would proponents of this theory explain the food chain — if one animal's source of food disappears, other animals in the food chain may be impacted and may, in fact, die?

4. According to Schnaiberg, the political economy of environmental problems and policies is shaped by modern industrial society's treadmill of production. This term refers to the inherent need of our economic system to continually yield profits by creating consumer demand for new products, even where this means expanding the ecosystem to its furthest limits. He argues that consumers are persuaded from early childhood to become part of a dominant materialistic culture in which personal identity depends on material possessions. What, if anything, is wrong with this? Do you think that Schnaiberg is referring to today's society or perhaps societies of the future?

Web Links

Dr. Michael D. Mehta: Environmental Sociology
http://arts.usask.ca/policynut/index4.htm
An excellent website complete with sound and graphics.

Canadian Environmental and Sustainable Development Research Capacity — Sociology
http://www.ec.gc.ca/erad/eng/sociology_e.cfm
Information from a host of Canadian authors that will enlighten you on the issue of sustainable development in Canada.

Global Recycling Network
http://grn.com/
Global Recycling Network is an electronic information exchange that specializes in the trade of recyclables and the marketing of eco-friendly products.

Recycling In Canada
http://www.recycle.nrcan.gc.ca/default_e.htm
The goal of this website is to promote and enhance recycling in Canada by providing information about metals recycling and recycling in general.

Solutions

True or False?

1. T
2. F
3. T
4. T
5. F
6. F
7. T
8. T
9. T
10. F

Multiple Choice

1. C
2. A
3. C
4. B
5. C
6. A
7. B
8. D
9. C
10. A
11. D
12. C
13. D
14. A
15. C

Chapter 17

Population, Aging, and Health

Chapter Introduction

I grew up in a pretty small city and have spent most of my life here. Last year, when I decided to go back to school for my doctorate, I had to commute to Toronto quite frequently. Many of my friends and family wondered why I just didn't move there to make my studies much easier. It didn't take me too long to reply to their questions and I told them that "there are too many people there for me!" I am very much a small town kind of person and could never imagine living in a city that has so many people walking down the streets, regardless of the time of day! Admittedly, I am not a world traveller and I often liken my excursions to OISE/UT to Dorothy as she finds herself outside of Kansas. I'm amazed when I see all of the people in the city and often wonder how many more our world can hold. Demographics are an essential part of sociological study. Since most of the work sociologists do involves human beings, it's incredibly important to study all aspects of them, and demography allows us to do that. For example, we know that the population of aging people in our society is growing. Do you notice this when you go out? If you're ever out shopping, take a look around you and see how many seniors are also out enjoying the day. It's probably not something that you would normally take notice of unless you were interested in the demographics of our country. Now that you've learned about this, make an effort to observe it on your next social outing.

In this chapter you'll learn the ways in which population is studied and how the world has grown over time. You'll also learn about the various theoretical perspectives that are used for analyzing the causes and consequences of population change. The chapter ends by looking at population trends in Canada, emphasizing the dynamics of mortality/health, fertility, and immigration and what their implications are on the size, age, and geographic distribution of the population.

Learning Objectives

At the conclusion of this chapter, you should be able to discuss or write about the following, without having to rely on the textbook:

1. The consideration of demographics — population size, growth, distribution, composition, fertility, mortality, and migration — is important to the study of societies as they change over time. Conversely, studies of changes or differences in fertility, mortality, and migration require sociological analysis.

2. Demography analyzes population states (size, geographical distribution, and composition by various characteristics) and population processes (fertility, mortality, and migration), their reciprocal influences, and their various determinants and consequences.

3. Malthus concluded that populations have a tendency to grow more rapidly than other resources and that it is important to control the growth of population by reducing births. Marx concluded that economic and social conditions determine the rate of population growth and that proper social arrangements should be able to accommodate population growth. Both of these perspectives are useful.

4. The demographic transition model summarizes the historical tendency of populations to move from an equilibrium of high birth rates and high death rates to one of low birth rates and low death rates. Because death rates decline sooner and faster than birth rates, there is considerable population expansion during the course of the transition. In the European populations, the demographic transition occurred mostly over the period 1750 to 1970, whereas in Asia, Latin America, and Africa, it started only in the 1950s.

5. Since Confederation, life expectancy in Canada has increased from 42 to 79 years as a result of higher standards of living, improvements in sanitation, and advances in medicine. Degenerative diseases have replaced infectious diseases as the major causes of death. In the same period, average births declined from seven to 1.5 births per woman, though the decline in fertility was not as uniform as the decline in mortality (the baby boom of the period 1946−66 represented a major exception to the downward trend). Average births now are fewer than would be needed for the long-term replacement of the population.

6. Immigration has contributed considerably to Canadian population growth. The net balance between immigration and emigration is responsible for close to a quarter of the population growth over the past century, and 18 percent of the current population is foreign born. Net migration in the period 1991−2001 accounted for 55 percent of the country's population growth. Immigration has brought significant ethnic diversity to Canada's population, including, since the mid-1960s, large numbers of arrivals from Asia, Latin America, and Africa. Controlling the level of immigration, particularly refugee arrivals, poses challenges in the context of demographic pressures at the world level.

7. Canada's population has grown rapidly since Confederation — twice as rapidly as the population of the world as a whole. Today, however, fertility is low, growth is less rapid, and the population is aging — a process that poses various challenges of adaptation, particularly in the areas of education, the labour force, health care, and pensions. At the same time, population distribution has tended to be very uneven, with different growth dynamics in the various regions. Movement has tended to be toward the western and southern parts of the country. In addition, immigrants have tended to concentrate in the three largest cities (Toronto, Montreal, and Vancouver). With the exception of Montreal, immigrants do not contribute to the relative size of the population of Quebec and the Atlantic provinces.

8. In terms of characteristics, Canada displays some unique features. Only 2.1 percent of the world population lives in countries with a higher life expectancy than Canada's, and only 10.3 percent in countries with lower fertility. In other ways, Canada shares in the slower population growth and consequent population aging that typically characterize the more developed countries and distinguish them from the younger and faster-growing populations of the developing world. Canada's relatively high and diversified immigration promotes a cultural mosaic that may help us to retain a common sense of destiny with the three-quarters of humanity that populate the less developed countries.

Quiz Questions

True or False?

1. Internal migration involves a new way of organizing human settlements that permits considerable growth in population.
   True or False

2. The higher mortality of lower-class men, due especially to heart disease, can be related to the stresses associated with their precarious economic situation, along with lack of social support for a healthy lifestyle, which can promote detrimental behaviour such as smoking, poor diet, and excessive drinking.
   True or False

3. According to Karl Marx, populations have a tendency to grow more rapidly than other resources and people can control the growth of population by reducing births.
   True or False

4. Some scholars have proposed that the rapid growth of the human species represents in biological terms a catastrophic event for the planet, comparable to an ice age or major meteoric collision.
   True or False

5. Population states and processes are dynamically interrelated. For instance, lower birth rates (a process) produce an older population (a state); conversely, an older population tends to have a lower birth rate.
   True or False

6. The population stock involves changes in population from one time to another as a function of births, deaths, and movements of people.
   True or False

7. Malthus argued that the capitalist class had a tendency not only to become more powerful as it came to exercise increasing control over the means of production, but also to become smaller in size.
   True or False

8. The mortality rate for lung cancer among women now exceeds that of breast cancer.
   True or False

9. Immigration clearly has a large impact on a population's age structure.
   True or False

10. The comparison of the relative health status of various sectors of the population permits an analysis of the differences across groups, and this points to the dynamics of well-being. For instance, men have a lower life expectancy than women, but women's advantage has shrunk from seven to five years.
    True or False

Multiple Choice

1. There has been a substantial long-term change in fertility, from about _____ births per woman in the 1850s to fewer than two births in the 1980s and the 1990s.

   a. 4

   b. 5

   c. 6

   d. 7

2. Demography does not involve the study of which of the following?

   a. cohabitation

   b. migration

   c. population composition

   d. fertility

3. The epidemiological transition involves four stages. Which of the following is not one of them?

   a. pestilence

   b. increasing trends towards better hygiene

   c. decline of infectious disease as the primary causes of death

   d. delayed degenerative diseases

4. According to Marx, the richer countries are becoming smaller in relative size, and the _____ system is becoming more dependent on cheap labour and raw materials from the rapidly growing populations of the Third World.

   a. socialist

   b. capitalist

   c. communist

   d. democratic

5. Which of the following is not a component of Canada's shifting demographic situation?

   a. increasing mortality

   b. low fertility

   c. low growth

   d. population aging

6. The _____ theory has been used to summarize the historical demographic experience of societies of European origin over the past two centuries, as well as the more recent experience of Third World societies.

   a. demographic transition

   b. migratory settlement

   c. immigration

   d. demographic patterning

7. _____ considered that the dynamics of population growth derived from the "mode of production" and the "relations of production," as these worked themselves out in specific stages of human history.
   a. Karl Marx
   b. Thomas Malthus
   c. Emile Durkheim
   d. David Foot

8. _____ is a broad perspective that embraces the subject of the causes and consequences of population processes.
   a. Social ecosystemics
   b. Demographic ecology
   c. Demographic patterning
   d. Human ecology

9. Political economist _____ developed a systematic theory of population change and its relation to economic conditions.
   a. John Maynard Keynes
   b. Adam Smith
   c. Thomas Malthus
   d. John Porter

10. The rate of roughly _____ births per woman has traditionally been viewed as the level of replacement fertility — that is, the level of fertility at which one generation will be fully replaced by the next.
    a. 2
    b. 3
    c. 4
    d. 5

11. Difficulties imposed by the environment can induce a population to find new forms of organization and technology that will enable it to survive and prosper — a process commonly known as _____.
    a. survival
    b. existence
    c. adaptation
    d. alteration

12. According to David Foot, analyzing human behaviour in terms of _____ produces actual data rather than misconceptions.
    a. age
    b. gender
    c. education
    d. occupation

13. In considering the distribution of the population over space, the analysis becomes more complex. Which of the following does not contribute to the complexity of the analysis?

    a. International immigrants tend to settle in certain parts of the country more than in others.

    b. Census polls do not account for illegal immigrants or transient people.

    c. Internal migration is not evenly distributed.

    d. Regions may differ in fertility and mortality rates.

14. Evidence from societies that until recently lived as hunters and gatherers suggests that the difficulty of finding soft food for children and the consequent need for long periods of lactation kept average births per woman in the range of _____.

    a. one or two

    b. three or four

    c. five or six

    d. six or seven

15. The _____ involved major changes in technology that fostered population growth; particularly important in this regard were developments that allowed resources to be extracted more efficiently from the environment.

    a. Industrial Revolution

    b. end of WWII

    c. invention of computer technology

    d. turn of the century

Critical Thinking

1. The Earth's population is constantly increasing. Some scholars believe that the rapid growth of the human species could result in a catastrophic event for the planet, comparable to an Ice Age. What are your thoughts on population growth? Do you think that population needs to be controlled? Why or why not? What measures could be taken to slow the rapid growth of the human population?

2. Weinfeld (1988) suggests there are two predominant visions that apply to immigration. One view sees Canada as well established and needing to protect its resources and its inheritance against destabilizing forces. In this view, tradition is preferable to change, and immigration policy should be cautious. The alternative perspective views Canada as a country that is young, rich, and not fully developed. From this perspective, immigration is part of a process of nation building; ethnic variety and demographic growth are interpreted positively. Which theory do you agree with and why?

3. Censuses were first taken to enable rulers to tax their citizens and to determine the number of men available for military service. I can remember when my mother took a part-time job as a census taker. I would tag along as she went from door to door and was often rewarded with a treat from one of the ladies in the neighbourhood. I often wonder how accurate those statistics were since much of the conversation between my mother and the neighbours had

little to do with the actual counting of people and more to do with what they were wearing or driving! How accurate do you think the census is? Would it be more reliable or valid if citizens were allowed to self-report?

4. Erlich and Erlich (1990) propose that rapid population growth, particularly at the world level and in poorer countries, is creating misery and poverty. Simon (1990) proposes that human capital is mainly what promotes economic growth and, consequently, that population growth increases our ability to solve the problems of hunger and poverty. Which theory do you most agree with? Why?

Web Links

Statistics Canada
http://www.statcan.ca/start.html
Statistics Canada generates statistics that help Canadians better understand their country — its population, resources, economy, society, and culture.

The International Society of Malthus Home Page
http://desip.igc.org/malthus/
The straight facts on this controversial thinker will shed new light on your opinion of his theories.

The Society for Human Ecology
http://www.societyforhumanecology.org/
The Society for Human Ecology (SHE) is an international interdisciplinary professional society that promotes the use of an ecological perspective in both research and application.

Making Sense of the Census
http://www.cbc.ca/news/indepth/background/census1.html
Finally, a website that can help you make sense of other statistically based websites, including the Census in Canada.

Solutions

True or False?

1. F

2. T

3. F

4. T

5. T

6. F

7. F

8. T

9. F

10. T

13. C

14. C

15. A

Multiple Choice

1. D

2. A

3. B

4. B

5. A

6. A

7. A

8. D

9. C

10. A

11. C

12. A

Chapter 18

Global Society

Chapter Introduction

I can't remember the first time that I actually thought of the world as a global community — can you? How often do you spend time thinking about the relationships that exist all over the world? It amazes me that technology has brought us to a point where people can simultaneously design and manufacture a piece of machinery when they are all in different countries. I can clearly remember my first conference call and I know it was a very different experience for me. I guess that I'm a visual person, and I had trouble following the conversation without being able to see with whom I was speaking. Do you drive a car that was built in another country? I once taught a student who refused to wear any clothing that wasn't made in Canada. I thought very highly of his dedication and commitment to the Canadian textile workers. This was well before the Kathie Lee Gifford scandal and the press coverage that surrounded that issue. We spoke about it at some length and he admitted that his selection in clothing was limited and he was often tempted to become a "victim of fashion" but he never did. I think that what was on the inside of his body was much more important to him than what was on the outside. In any event, that student reminds me that the occurrences that take place far away from us can still affect us close to home. It's amazing how something that happens a million miles away can affect the way that we live our everyday lives and, if you stop to think about it, it's amazing at how often it happens.

In this chapter you'll realize that globalization creates controversy among sociologists, as well as provoking political and public concerns. Additionally, you'll learn that the study of the global economy is a relatively recent phenomenon. By seeing the world as a "global village" you'll see that the future of the world depends on the shape and direction of global agendas.

Learning Objectives

At the conclusion of this chapter, you should be able to discuss or write about the following, without having to rely on the textbook:

1. Western expansion and consciousness of threats to the globe as a whole have added the new idea of a global society to the old one of world society.

2. Globalization may be seen as ushering in a new historical period and creating a level of social organization beyond that of the nation-state.

3. The end of the Cold War has resulted not in a unitary power centre for the world but in a new sense of interdependence and a perceived weakness of the nation-state.

4. Although the world economy has become a single transnational system, globalization may nonetheless promote local production.

5. The people of the world travel and communicate across national borders as never before, lifting social relationships out of their local contexts.

6. Global images and information from the mass media enhance global consciousness and facilitate the development of a new globalist social movement.

7. Globalization can impinge on people's everyday lives in ways that create anxiety and insecurity, and cause them to re-evaluate their identity and lifestyle.

8. Homogenization and hybridization are equally possible outcomes of globalization.

9. Because of reactions against globalization, there is no guarantee that a global society will realize its full promise. Much depends on whether the benefits of globalization can be distributed more justly throughout the world.

Quiz Questions

True or False?

1. Although Paris is the capital city of a state whose economy is relatively minor in today's world league, it is the world's largest foreign exchange transaction centre, as well as being second only to Tokyo as a banking centre.
   True or False

2. Roland Robertson, the first scholar to make globalization a sociological theme, described globalization as a concept that refers to both the compression of the world and the intensification of the world as a whole. The processes and actions to which the concept of globalization now refers have been proceeding with some interruptions for many centuries, but the main focus of discussion of globalization is on relatively recent themes.
   True or False

3. When Marshall McLuhan (1962) announced that the "new electronic interdependence recreates in the image of a global village," he used the word "global" in a new way to highlight the worldwide direct communication, transmission, and reception of speech and images. The world, or many worlds, now entered one's own locality.
   True or False

4. The internal-combustion engine and the computer work in the same way in Tokyo as they do in New York and bring with them similar consequences for ways of living. This phenomenon is called globalization — the idea that all societies are taking on the same characteristics.
   True or False

5. Anthony Giddens (1990) emphasizes the notion of disembedding, which occurs when people increasingly put their faith in abstract systems that were organized over the course of decades, span thousands of kilometres, and involve millions of people.
   True or False

6. The world political system has developed as the empire of a super-state as well as a single world state. It has thereby become a forum for global consciousness, where opinions are formed and conflicts resolved by hammering out common global interests.
   True or False

7. Immanuel Wallerstein (1974) has made the development of the world economy the theme of his world-system theory, which considers economic relations only from the perspective of the world as a whole, with states representing merely one force among many.
   True or False

8. International trade is a set of contradictory processes that focuses our attention on the prospects for a global society and culture. It causes us to revisit the theme of the possibilities of humankind, which was long obscured while sociology was dominated by the concerns of the nation-state.
True or False

9. Theories of postmodernity argue that contrary to modernist claims, society is culturally fragmented rather than homogenous, lacking direction toward "progress" or any other single goal.
True or False

10. The world economy has become a single transnational system; however, globalization may promote local economic activity rather than concentrate it in one or a few locations.
True or False

Multiple Choice

1. The term "globalization" came into widespread use among social scientists, and later, in the mass media only in the _____.
    a. 1960s
    b. 1970s
    c. 1980s
    d. 1990s

2. Which of the following is not one of the elements of a global economy?
    a. international economic institutions such as the International Monetary Fund
    b. a worldwide division of labour and class system
    c. a global system of communication
    d. the global spread of new production practices and consumption patterns

3. Modern means of transportation allow people and goods to travel once-unthinkable distances; telephones make it possible to talk to someone on the other side of the world; satellites beam images all over the world; recording technology enables us to preserve voices and images of people from the past. All this amounts to what Harvey (1989) calls _____.
    a. trans-world linkage
    b. trans-corporate technology
    c. global networking
    d. time-space compression

4. The processes and actions to which the concept of globalization now refers have been proceeding with some interruptions for many centuries, but the main focus of discussion of globalization is on relatively recent times. Robertson (1992) suggests that the world has become one place but our awareness of it as one place, while also intensified, is a distinct issue. By interruptions, he makes it clear that _____.

   a. globalization is not some irresistible force

   b. the transformations that are presently occurring are inevitable

   c. globalization depends on human actions

   d. the focus on recent globalization is itself new

5. The twin impact of growing numbers of immigrants and refugees is especially evident in Germany. At the end of 1999 there were _____ foreign residents in the federal republic, constituting 8.9 percent of the total population.

   a. 2.4 million

   b. 4.6 million

   c. 5.9 million

   d. 7.3 million

6. According to Hall (1992) the fragmentation of _____ leaves people free to make up their own minds, choose their own style, and find their own identity. As a result, old identities are replaced by new hybrids.

   a. communication

   b. society

   c. culture

   d. technology

7. Which of the following forces did not impel the expansion of the West?

   a. universalism

   b. imperialism

   c. capitalism

   d. positivism

8. Science has not only produced innovations that have worldwide application, it has also become aware of the consequences of their use for the world. The interdependence of the world combines with the scientific knowledge of the modern period to produce what Beck (1992) has called _____.

   a. global challenge

   b. ethic/nation debate

   c. global risk

   d. global dilemma

9. The globalization of capital is not simply a matter of large organizations gaining ever-increasing control over the world's economy. With globalization, the chances for people to accumulate vast personal fortunes have also increased. This new class of people is referred to as the _____.

    a. nouveau riche

    b. international elite

    c. global trendsetters

    d. international untouchables

10. When Filipinos sing American popular songs, they are not returning to an earlier America but creating a yearning for something they never had. Arjun Appadurai (1996) calls this _____.

    a. nostalgia without memory

    b. false memory syndrome

    c. inherited memories

    d. foreign media influence

11. The idea that human beings belong to single species and that their relations with each other bind them into humankind is as old as written history. Yet it is only in the last _____ years that we have talked about this in terms of globalization.

    a. 5

    b. 10

    c. 15

    d. 20

12. Sociologists have sought to adapt their thinking to take account of ecology as a global concern. For Ulrich Beck (1992), this has meant thinking of society in terms of response to _____, rather than in terms of the distribution of wealth.

    a. technology

    b. risk

    c. postmodernity

    d. globalization

13. We can identify three forces that have impelled the expansion of the West. Which of the following is not one of them?

    a. universalism

    b. relativism

    c. imperialism

    d. capitalism

14. _____ (1991) suggests that globalization forces individuals into a process of self-inquiry because the fundamental indeterminacy of the world creates anxiety and insecurity: "The more tradition loses its hold, and the more daily life is reconstituted in terms of the dialectical interplay of the local and the global, the more individuals are forced to negotiate lifestyle choices among a diversity of options."

    a. David Foot

    b. Anthony Giddens

    c. Tony Blair

    d. David Suzuki

15. People who share an interest today can communicate instantly worldwide over the Internet. They can use the Internet to discuss business, scientific research, political views, sex, or rare birds. This new form of community is known as a _____.

    a. multi-domain community

    b. cyber-social community

    c. virtual community

    d. global network community

Critical Thinking

1. A central difference between Robertson and Giddens lies in their causal ordering of events. Giddens considers modernity to be a cause of globalization. He thus focuses on how new technologies of communication have helped globalize the world. For Robertson, however, the causal sequence is the other way around: Modernity, he says, is the result of globalization. Thus, focusing on institutions of social order at the global level and values that focus on globality, Robertson traces their origins back at least 2000 years, long before the modern era. This is a lot like the old "chicken and egg" riddle that has been around for ages. If you really thought about the views of both of these theorists though, which one makes more sense for you? If you had to participate in a debate and focus on either Robertson or Giddens, who would you choose and how would you defend your argument?

2. Large corporations with international undertakings stand accused of social injustice, unfair labour practices — including slave labour wages, living and working conditions — as well as a lack of concern for the environment, mismanagement of natural resources, and ecological change. Anti-globalization demonstrations have achieved worldwide support partly because they target, per se, its representatives and its effects are global in nature. Major brand names, among them Nike, Starbucks, McDonald's, and Shell Oil, are principal targets. Many of these corporations have been connected to celebrity actors or athletes. The Kathie Lee Gifford incident was the cause of massive demonstrations worldwide as she was accused of running sweatshops and abusing child labour laws in order to manufacture her clothing line. Do you think that the conditions under which many labourers work would have gone on unnoticed if not for her celebrity status? To what degree do you think it still goes on in the world?

3. The threat of global political domination by media conglomerates is of great concern today since the capacity to influence opinion worldwide is now open to them and it lies beyond the scope of political leaders who work within the confines of nation-states. A global cultural hegemony exercised by media moguls is not what those who want a peaceful world order have advocated. What are the implications of a shift in power to the media? Do you think that actual coverage of world events would be more objective if the media had more power?

4. I was totally mesmerized by combinations of offspring that might result from the mating of seven men and women of various racial and ethnic backgrounds, as depicted in the *Time Magazine* photo on page 487. I wonder how accurate it really is. Do you believe what you see? What if the computer generation became so advanced that you could see pictures of your child at various stages of his or her life, before he or she was already born? Would you use this service?

Web Links

Postmodernism: Boundaryless Self in a Boundaryless World
http://it.stlawu.edu/~pomo/mike/index.html
Here's a look at postmodernism and the implications of this theoretical model for the global society.

Globalization: Index
http://globalization.icaap.org/
An excellent page to add to your favourites, which will act as an informative, easy, and highly accessible link to global issues.

Trade and Globalization
http://www.epinet.org/subjectpages/trade.cfm
Sponsored by the Economic Policy Institute, this site offers a wealth of academic research in this area.

The Official Site of Marshall McLuhan
http://www.marshallmcluhan.com/
More about one of the great thinkers in the development of globalization theories.

Solutions

True or False?

1. F
2. F
3. T
4. F
5. T
6. F
7. T
8. F
9. T
10. T

Multiple Choice

1. C
2. C
3. D
4. B
5. D
6. C
7. D
8. C
9. B
10. A
11. D
12. B
13. B
14. B
15. C

Chapter 19

Deviance and Crime

Chapter Introduction

Things have really changed since I was an undergraduate student many years ago. I would have never thought of going to class with blue hair or a pierced eyebrow. Now that I'm teaching undergraduate students, those things that I once thought were wildly deviant are just a normal part of everyday life in college. This is one of my favourite topics to teach because everyone has such a different notion of what is and what is not deviant. Many times when people think of someone who is deviant, they think of a criminal or someone who has done something horrible. Often we don't realize that deviance has many forms — an incredibly gifted child, an extraordinary athlete, or a man wearing a kilt are all examples of how we define deviance in society, and if you think about it, you realize that deviants are not always the bad guys! Deviance occurs in all societies but is not necessarily defined or socially constructed the same in each culture. For example, a man wearing a kilt may not be seen as deviant in Scotland, but he may get a couple of odd looks in Canada. When I think of deviance, I always remember the old adage — "one man's junk is another man's treasure". Deviance, because it is a social construction, can take on different forms and different meanings in all societes.

This chapter discusses the different ways in which sociologists have thought about deviance. You'll learn that some are interested primarily in where rules about deviance come from, how and why these rules change, and the consequences of labelling people or behaviours as deviant. You'll also see that other theorists focus on why some people tend to become rule-breakers. Making that important connection between theory and reality, the final part of this chapter looks at recent trends in Canada as well as changes in crime and social control around the world. A central theme of this chapter is that deviance is not simply about marginal people and odd behaviours. Studying how deviance is defined and how people react to it tells us about how a society is organized: how power, privilege, and resources are distributed and how social order is achieved. As you are probably already aware, there's a lot more to deviance than meets the eye!

Learning Objectives

At the conclusion of this chapter, you should be able to discuss or write about the following, without having to rely on the textbook:

1. Deviance and crime are defined by the social reactions to them. Both what is defined as deviance and the way people react to deviance depend on social circumstances. Even what you may consider to be serious deviance is subject to conflicting opinions and changing social relations.

2. Crime is a special case of deviance and is defined by social norms that are formalized in criminal law. The response to crime is through formal social control — such as the criminal justice and correctional systems — whereas the response to non-criminal deviance is through informal social control — such as gossip, avoidance, and other forms of disapproval. There tends to be wide — though certainly not complete — agreement that crime is wrong, but much less agreement that non-criminal forms of deviance are wrong.

3. Deviance is defined through a political process that typically involves struggles between competing groups over status, resources, knowledge, and power. While there is often some relationship between the harm that a behaviour causes and the likelihood that the behaviour is defined as deviance, many harmful behaviours are not defined as deviant and some behaviours defined as deviant are not harmful.

4. Sociological explanations of deviant behaviour can be grouped into two types: those that emphasize the social factors that motivate or allow people to engage in deviance, and those that emphasize the political processes and power relations that result in some people and behaviours being defined and treated as deviant while others are not.

5. Rates of crimes have increased in Canada in recent years. Canadians are less likely to be victims of serious violent crime than people in the United States, but face higher risks of homicide than citizens of other developed democracies. Aboriginal Canadians are at particularly high risk of involvement in criminal homicide — both as victims and as offenders. They are also overrepresented among those incarcerated in Canadian prisons and jails. This has been attributed in part to systemic racism in the criminal justice system.

6. Crime rates are often affected by major social changes. For example, rapidly changing technologies have created new opportunities for both personal and property crime and the globalization of the world's economy has been accompanied by the globalization of corporate and organized crime. Changes in gender inequalities, on the other hand, have not reduced the gender gap in criminal offences. Men still greatly outnumber women among offenders.

7. Canada has traditionally favoured the crime-control model of the criminal process and, consistent with that model, relies heavily on incarceration. More recently, however, this emphasis has shifted. With the introduction of the Charter of Rights and Freedoms, the due-process model has gained ground. And while Canada continues to incarcerate offenders at higher rates than most other Western democracies, Canadian incarceration rates have declined in recent years as the criminal justice system explores alternatives to imprisonment.

Quiz Questions

True or False?

1. Early childhood socialization — the ways in which parents reward and discipline their children's behaviour and the extent to which they develop affectionate bonds with them — is critical to all control theories. If those controls are developed early in life, children will not be as susceptible to the deviant influences of peers, nor will they respond to strain with deviant actions.
   True or False

2. Nonconformity becomes deviant when it produces a negative social reaction and when there are concerted public efforts to change the behaviour or punish the person. These efforts are what many sociologists call sanctions and they can take many forms.
   True or False

3. The effort to get human rights coverage extended to gay men and lesbians was first successful in Quebec in 1977. Active opposition meant that almost 20 years had passed before the federal government added sexual orientation to the list of protected categories in its human

rights legislation of 1996. Same-sex marriage became legal in Canada in 1998, but only after decades of political and legal battles.
True or False

4. While the primary goal of the due process model is reducing crime and protecting society by granting legal officials broad powers, the crime control model emphasizes the protection of legal rights of the accused to ensure justice.
    True or False

5. Opportunity theories do not try to explain why people decide to commit crime. They simply assume that many people lack the controls to stop them. Opportunity theories connect the potential offender described by control theories to particular offences.
    True or False

6. Because it is social reactions and social controls that define deviance, many sociologists contend that understanding the political processes and power relations that create definitions of deviance and determine to whom those definitions are applied is the key to explaining deviance.
    True or False

7. Sociological explanations of deviance can be grouped into two types: those that emphasize the social factors that motivate or allow people to engage in deviance, and those that emphasize the political processes and power relations that result in some individuals and behaviours being defined and treated as deviant while others are not.
    True or False

8. Some learning theories argue that long exposure to violent images desensitizes young people to violence and conveys the message that violence is an acceptable way to respond to frustration.
    True or False

9. Contrary to public perceptions about youth violence, the average age of those accused of homicide has decreased in Canada since the 1970s, and is currently 32 years.
    True or False

10. While Canadians are more likely than Americans to be the victims of burglaries and car thefts, they are much less likely than Americans to be the victims of serious violent crime, such as aggravated assault, robbery, and homicide.
    True or False

Multiple Choice

1. Although deviance is defined by negative social reactions, it can have positive consequences for some social groups. This notion was an important theme of _____ work. He reasoned that they must serve some positive social function.

    a. Emile Durkheim's
    b. Karl Marx's
    c. Robert Merton's
    d. Max Weber's

2. According to the _____ perspective, the various social, economic, political, ethnic, religious and professional groups that characterize modern societies continually compete with each other for status and influence.

    a. institutional competition

    b. social conflict

    c. status conflict

    d. laissez-faire

3. Native people account for _____ of all persons arrested for homicide in Canada, according to the Canadian Centre for Justice Statistics. Police agencies in Canada do not publish or analyze data on ethic and cultural backgrounds of those arrested, and so it has been difficult for researchers to determine whether other groups are overrepresented among arrestees.

    a. 5%

    b. 10%

    c. 25%

    d. 35%

4. Many people feel that the criminal law on homicide should apply to a wider array of acts, such as abortion or deaths caused by the negligence of corporations. The controversy over Saskatchewan farmer _____ second-degree murder conviction and life sentence illustrates the debates that can take place over what types of killings should be punished.

    a. Daniel Brown's

    b. Robert Latimer's

    c. John Wayne Gacy's

    d. Clifford Olson's

5. An important contribution of critical perspectives on deviance is their focus on the consequences for the people and the groups who are targets of the deviance defining process. The _____ perspective is organized around the idea that societal reactions to deviance are an important cause of the deviance.

    a. labelling

    b. stigma

    c. differential association

    d. blaming the victim

6. _____ are variations in lifestyle that help make our lives more interesting and, at times, more exciting; the fads and fashions of speech, appearance, and play are examples of these.

    a. Deviant acts

    b. Breaking the rules

    c. White lies

    d. Social diversions

7. There are at least three ways in which learning theories can be applied to explain deviant behaviour. Which of the following is not one of them?

   a. Long exposure to violent images desensitizes young people to violence and conveys the message that violence is an acceptable way to respond to frustration.

   b. Some individuals, regardless of their social status or gender, are genetically predisposed to engaging in criminal behaviour.

   c. Many types of crime require opportunities to learn specific techniques and procedures.

   d. Many crimes are simply the imitation or modelling of others' behaviour.

8. Crime that is committed by legitimate business organizations includes violations of anti-trust, environmental, food and drug, tax, health and safety, and corruption laws is called corporate crime. The economic costs of these crimes have been estimated at _____times those associated with street crimes.

   a. 20

   b. 30

   c. 40

   d. 50

9. Before the _____ century, centralized states either did not exist or were not strong enough to sponsor the institutions of formal social control that predominate in modern societies. With the growth of market-based economies and industrialization, state-based formal social controls emerged.

   a. 16th

   b. 17th

   c. 18th

   d. 19th

10. The Youth Criminal Justice Act allows an adult sentence for any youth aged _____ and older convicted of a serious crime, increases the scope of cases for which youths can presumptively receive an adult sentence, lowers the age at which youths found guilty of certain offences will presumptively be sentenced as adults, and permits judges to consider allowing the publication of names of some youths found guilty of serious violent offences even if they were not given the adult sentence.

    a. 13

    b. 14

    c. 15

    d. 16

11. _____ incarcerates more people per capita than most industrialized countries, but is increasingly relying on alternatives to incarceration for less serious criminal offences.

    a. The United States

    b. Canada

    c. Sweden

    d. Denmark

12. In August 2002, a woman in _____ received a sentence of death by stoning, a punishment prescribed for adultery under some versions of law. The sentence is to be carried out in 2004 after she has finished weaning the baby who was used as proof of her adultery at trial.
    a. Nigeria
    b. Iran
    c. Iraq
    d. Egypt

13. The public is becoming more aware of the high cost of imprisonment. Canada spends well over $2 billion on adult and youth corrections. For example, in 1999–2000 it cost roughly _____ per year to keep one person in a federal prison in Canada.
    a. $32 000
    b. $41 000
    c. $55 000
    d. $67 000

14. One example of a _____ is the campaign by Mothers Against Drunk Driving (MADD) to educate the public about the costs of drunk driving, to stigmatize those who drink and drive, and to increase criminal penalties for drunk driving.
    a. lobby group
    b. moral crusade
    c. social organization
    d. political faction

15. For _____ theorists, conflict between different classes, and the desire of the capitalist class to control the working class results in some behaviours (such as burglary) being targeted for control more than other behaviours (such as corporate crime).
    a. functional
    b. strain
    c. Marxist
    d. symbolic interaction

Critical Thinking

1. Informal social control occurs in interactions among individuals and includes expressions of disapproval, avoidance, and the many other ways we try to communicate and enforce standards of appropriate behaviour in our everyday lives. All of us have been stopped from doing something by an internal voice asking, "What would others think?" That is informal social control in action. Why do you think that this "inner voice" is stronger in some than in others? What sort of things would affect your "inner voice"? How often do you listen to your "inner voice"?

2. Efforts to define and punish deviance have other costs. Gary Marx (1981) identifies a number of ways in which these efforts actually produce more deviance. For example, high-speed chases by police have resulted in serious injuries and deaths of bystanders, often leading to

manslaughter charges against people who otherwise would have faced less serious charges. Efforts to control deviance can often have unintended and harmful consequences for individuals and society as a whole. How can we keep a better balance between deviant behaviour and the conforming behaviours that have fewer negative effects on society in general?

3. The success of the MADD campaign reflects the group's ability to gain the support of the media and various politicians, through which both legal and popular definitions of drunk driving were changed. Do you think that groups such as this one would be as successful if they didn't have the support of the media? How would you begin to effectively lobby for a social cause?

4. The National Association to Advance Fat Acceptance, the Living Large Club, and the Ample Opportunity Group urge their members and the public to question the social intolerance of obesity. Similarly, in response to their increasingly deviant identity, some smokers are aggressively contesting their stigmatization. In a society that celebrates the diversity of all kinds of people, how do we determine the distinction between someone who is different and someone who is deviant? Do you think that some groups are getting carried away with their causes?

Web Links

Bureau of Justice Statistics — Corrections Statistics
http://www.ojp.usdoj.gov/bjs/correct.htm
Use this site to compare American crime statistics with those in Canada.

Justice and Crime
http://www.statcan.ca/english/Pgdb/justic.htm
Use this site to compare Canadian crime statistics with those in the United States.

Canadian Centre for Justice — Statistics Profile Series
http://www.statcan.ca/english/freepub/85F0033MIE/free.htm
A great website to go back in time and see how the trends in deviance have changed.

MADD Canada — News
http://www.madd.ca/news/n000812.htm
A great example of the power of moral crusades.

Solutions

True or False?

1. T
2. F
3. F
4. F
5. T
6. T
7. T
8. T
9. F
10. T

Multiple Choice

1. A
2. C
3. C
4. B
5. A
6. D
7. B
8. D
9. B
10. B
11. B
12. A
13. D
14. B
15. C

Chapter 20

Politics and Social Movements

Chapter Introduction

Have you ever participated in a rally or peace protest? Are you a registered voter and have you exercised your right to vote? Can you see yourself leading a demonstration outside the Parliament buildings? Politics and social movements often go hand in hand and both are integral parts of studying sociology. If you've ever been involved in or volunteered for a political campaign, you probably have a good idea of the massive amount of time, work, and money that goes into every election. Are you a politically minded person who follows politics closely, or are you someone who is relatively apathetic. It seems to me that people fall into one of two groups when it comes to politics. On one side there are those who are avidly political and aware of what's going on in Canada and around the world, and then there are those that fall into the less enthusiastic or apathetic category. These are the people who feel that they don't know enough about politics to make an informed choice on a candidate and because they don't want to spoil a ballot, they don't vote. Of course, I could be totally wrong on this one, but this is the way that it appears to me. How would you categorize Canadians in terms of political awareness? Does it surprise you that the United States has a very low turnout for voters? I've always considered the States to be an extremely patriotic nation, but results from recent research don't indicate that.

In this chapter, you'll learn that the power of a group may be widely recognized as legitimate or valid under some circumstances. If it is, raw power becomes legitimate authority. Weber's typology of authority has three bases: traditional, legal rational, and charismatic. The people who occupy the command posts of institutions are generally seen as authorities. Under other circumstances, however, power flows to non-authorities. This undermines the legitimacy of authority. In this case, non-authorities form social movements or collective attempts to change part or all of the social order. They may riot, petition, strike, demonstrate, and establish pressure groups, unions, and political parties in order to achieve their aims. Additionally, you'll learn how politics has developed over the past 300 years and what you can reasonably expect in the near future.

Learning Objectives

At the conclusion of this chapter, you should be able to discuss or write about the following, without having to rely on the textbook:

1. Democracy involves a two-way process of control between the state (the set of institutions that formulate and carry out a country's law, policies, and binding regulations) and civil society (the private sphere, consisting of social movements, political parties, etc.).

2. The level of democracy in a society depends on the capability of civil society to influence the state through citizen support of social movements, political parties, and other groups. That capacity increases as power becomes more widely distributed in society.

3. While pluralists are correct to note that democratic politics is about negotiation and compromise, they fail to appreciate how advantaged groups tend to have more political influence.

4. While elitist theories are correct to note that power is concentrated in the hands of advantaged groups, they fail to appreciate how variations in the distribution of power influence political behaviour and public policy.

5. While power-balance theorists focus on the effect of changes in the distribution of power in society, they fail to appreciate what state-centred theorists emphasize — that state institutions and laws also affect political behaviour and public policy.

6. The degree to which power is widely distributed influences the success of particular kinds of parties and policies. Widely distributed power is associated with the success of labour parties and policies that redistribute wealth.

7. Research does not support the view that social movements emerge when relative deprivation spreads.

8. Research does suggest that people are more inclined to rebel against the status quo when they are bound by close social ties to many other people who feel similarly wronged and when they have the money and other resources needed to protest.

9. In order for social movements to grow, members must engage in frame alignment, making the activities, goals, and ideology of the movement congruent with the interests, beliefs, and values of potential new recruits.

10. The history of democracy is a struggle for the acquisition of constantly broadening citizenship rights — first the right to free speech, freedom of religion, and justice before the law, then the right to vote and run for office, then the right to a certain level of economic security and full participation in the life of society, and finally, the right of marginal groups to full citizenship and the right of humanity as a whole to peace and security.

11. In the Third World, social movements have focused less on broadening the bases of democracy than on ensuring more elemental human rights, notably freedom from colonial rule and freedom to create the conditions for independent economic growth. In some cases these movements have taken extreme, anti-democratic forms.

Quiz Questions

True or False?

1. Marx predicted that capitalism would drive business owners into bankruptcy and peasants into the cities. Marx thought that in the cities huge masses of workers would become class-conscious and solidarity would be born.
   True or False

2. People are more inclined to rebel against the status quo when they are bound by close social ties to other people who feel similarly wronged and when they have the money and other resources needed to protest.
   True or False

3. Power is exercised in all social settings, from the family to the classroom to the workplace. However, the ultimate seat of power in society is in its political leaders, as their authority stands

above all others, and if they need to use force to maintain order or protect their countries' borders, most people will regard their actions as legitimate.
True or False

4. Normal politics is politics as it is practised when authorities are firmly in power. Politics beyond the rules is politics as it is practised when the legitimacy of authority grows weak.
True or False

5. The level of democracy in a society depends on the capacity of citizens to influence the state through their support of political parties, social movements, and other groups. That capacity decreases, however, as power becomes more widely distributed in society.
True or False

6. With the exception of Switzerland, the United States has the lowest voter turnout of any democracy in the world.
True or False

7. About 85% of Swedish citizens vote in federal elections, compared to about 65% in Canada. That is mainly because working-class Swedes are more likely to vote than working-class Canadians.
True or False

8. Many surveys show that political involvement increases with social class. The likelihood of phoning or writing a member of Parliament, helping a candidate in an election campaign, contributing money to a political party, and running for office increases steeply as one moves up the class hierarchy.
True or False

9. Elite theorists argue that the distribution of power in society does change, sometimes massively. They admit that power is usually concentrated in the hands of the wealthy but they also note that other classes sometimes gain power. This has big implications for political life. Among other things, the distribution of power determines how democratic a society is.
True or False

10. State-centred theory is one interpretation of the relationship between state and civil society. According to state-centred theorists, we live in a heterogeneous society with many competing interests and centres of power.
True or False

Multiple Choice

1. _____ is the process by which individual interests, beliefs, and values either become congruent and complementary with the activities, ideas, and goals of the movement or fail to do so.
    a. Congruence theory
    b. Resource mobilization theory
    c. Social alignment theory
    d. Frame alignment theory

2. According to Weber's typology, which of the following is not a base of authority?

    a. traditional authority

    b. charismatic authority

    c. educational authority

    d. legal-rational authority

3. John Porter's classic, *The Vertical Mosaic*, was the first in a series of Canadian studies that demonstrate the weaknesses of pluralism and corroborate some aspects of elite theory. These studies show that roughly_____ of Canadian prime ministers, premiers, and cabinet ministers were born into the richest 10% of families in the country.

    a. 10%

    b. 20%

    c. 30%

    d. 40%

4. Some Marxists, known as "instrumentalists," criticize the basic tenets of elite theory. They say that elites form a ruling class dominated by big business and that the state is, for example, an arm of the business elite. According to the Marxist theorists, which of the following is not a critique of elite theory?

    a. Members of wealthy families occupy important state positions in highly disproportionate numbers.

    b. Government officials rely mainly on the representatives of big business for advice.

    c. Citizens continue to purchase the goods and services that perpetuate the success of big businesses.

    d. Political parties rely mainly on big business for financial support.

5. Only in the United States do individual citizens have to take the initiative to go out and register themselves in voter registration centres. As a result, the United States has a proportionately smaller pool of eligible voters than the other democracies. Only about _____ of American citizens are registered to vote.

    a. 23%

    b. 34%

    c. 48%

    d. 65%

6. New social movements are novel in that they attract a disproportionately large number of highly educated, well-to-do people from the social, educational, and cultural fields. Such people are predisposed to participate for several reasons. Which of the following is not one of them?

    a. They have more access to and are more familiar with the use of various forms of media that create an awareness of social causes.

    b. Their higher education exposes them to radical ideas and makes those ideas appealing.

    c. They tend to hold jobs outside the business community, which often opposes their values.

    d. They often get personally involved in the problems of their clients and audiences, sometimes even becoming their advocates.

7. Social movements often used their power to expand the rights of citizens. Which is not a stage in this process?

    a. civil citizenship

    b. legal citizenship

    c. social citizenship

    d. political citizenship

8. By means of demonstrating, petitioning, and gaining the support of influential liberal-minded men, women won the right to vote in all of Canada in _____.

    a. 1918

    b. 1925

    c. 1940

    d. 1945

9. The women's movement operates at both the grassroots level and within established political organizations to achieve its aim. It contains internal divisions, comprised of women of all theoretical backgrounds. Which of the following is not one of them?

    a. Liberal feminists

    b. Conservative feminists

    c. Radical feminists

    d. Socialist feminists

10. In Sweden, over three-quarters of blue-collar and white-collar workers are union members. In Canada, only about a third of workers are members of unions. Which of the following is not a consequence of this?

    a. Swedish governments have acted more vigorously than Canadian governments to eradicate poverty and equalize incomes.

    b. The Swedish socialist party has formed the government almost continuously since WWII. In contrast, Canada's socialist party, the NDP, has never formed the federal government or even had a representative in the federal cabinet.

    c. Since Canada's population is aging so rapidly, many seniors do not have the mobility to make it to the polls to vote, and fail to represent their political opinions.

    d. Since women are disproportionately concentrated in low-income, low-status jobs, they benefit more than men where the working class is more powerful.

11. _____ theorists teach us that, despite the concentration of power in society, substantial shifts in the distribution of power do occur, and they have discernible effects on voting patterns and public policies.

    a. Power-balance

    b. Elite

    c. State-centered

    d. Pluralist

12. Sociologists have compared measures of relative deprivation with the frequency of demonstrations, strikes, and acts of collective violence in France, Italy, Germany, and England. They have found that, in general, outbreaks of collective unrest do not _____ with mounting relative deprivation.
    a. increase
    b. decrease
    c. change
    d. occur

13. _____ occurs when people experience an intolerable gap between the social rewards they think they deserve and the social rewards that they expect to receive.
    a. Social disharmony
    b. Relative deprivation
    c. Equitable disruption
    d. Status conflict

14. Research shows that in Canada, since WWII, strike activity has been high when certain societal conditions exist. Which of the following is not one of them?
    a. a recent increase in the cost of living
    b. unemployment is low
    c. union membership is high
    d. governments have shown themselves to be generous in their provision of social welfare benefits

15. The globalization of social movements was facilitated by the ease with which people in various national movements could travel and communicate with like-minded activists from other countries. In 1953, there were about 110 international social movement organizations. By 1993, there were over _____.
    a. 500
    b. 550
    c. 600
    d. 650

Critical Thinking

1. In Canada and other democracies, working-class and poor people are less likely to vote than members of the middle and upper classes. They are also less likely to contact their elected representatives, contribute to election campaigns, and run for office. Only people with high incomes, substantial wealth, and postsecondary education have the time, money, and social connections required for the most intense forms of political engagement. What does this tell you about our elected officials? How does this class bias affect how we are governed?

2. By now you've probably learned a whole lot about Canada and many other countries that make our world abound with diversity. In terms of politics and government, how democratic is the Canadian state? Does the interaction between state and civil society ensure that every

citizen has a roughly equal say in the determination of law and policies? Do you think that some citizens are just a little more equal than others? Or do you think that some citizens are a lot more equal than others?

3. Certainly, in any given election, the entire eligible population does not vote. Have you ever voted in a federal, provincial, or municipal election? If not, perhaps you have voted in a school election. Some people think that their vote can't change a thing, and others feel that they don't know enough about politics to cast their vote, so they don't bother voting at all. How much importance do you place on voting? Why? What measures could be taken to ensure greater voting participation?

4. If you have not already done so, would you participate in a rally or protest? How strong would your beliefs have to be in order to formally protest against something? What type of cause are you more likely to support? Does the type of support you offer (for example, time or monetary donation) depend on the cause that you're willing to support?

Web Links

NCPA: Government and Politics — Influence of Liberal Lobby Groups
http://www.ncpa.org/pd/govern/pd120999e.html
Presented by the National Center for Policy Analysis, this website includes recent information on the political state of the economy — mostly American information.

Political History and Evolution: Your Canadian Election Headquarters
http://www.elect.ca/evolution.php
A great site on the political history of Canada. Test your knowledge on the Canadian Trivia Quiz.

International Centre for Human Rights and Democratic Development
http://www.ichrdd.ca/frame2.iphtml?langue=0
Useful information on human rights and international political movements from around the world.

Democracy Watch Homepage
http://www.dwatch.ca/
Democracy Watch is Canada's leading citizen group advocating democratic reform, government accountability, and corporate responsibility.

Solutions

True or False?

1. T
2. T
3. F
4. T
5. F
6. T
7. T
8. F
9. T
10. F

Multiple Choice

1. D
2. C
3. D
4. C
5. D
6. A
7. B
8. C
9. B
10. C
11. A
12. A
13. B
14. A
15. C